SpringerBriefs in Education

We are delighted to announce SpringerBriefs in Education, an innovative product type that combines elements of both journals and books. Briefs present concise summaries of cutting-edge research and practical applications in education. Featuring compact volumes of 50 to 125 pages, the SpringerBriefs in Education allow authors to present their ideas and readers to absorb them with a minimal time investment. Briefs are published as part of Springer's eBook Collection. In addition, Briefs are available for individual print and electronic purchase.

SpringerBriefs in Education cover a broad range of educational fields such as: Science Education, Higher Education, Educational Psychology, Assessment & Evaluation, Language Education, Mathematics Education, Educational Technology, Medical Education and Educational Policy.

SpringerBriefs typically offer an outlet for:

- An introduction to a (sub)field in education summarizing and giving an overview of theories, issues, core concepts and/or key literature in a particular field
- A timely report of state-of-the art analytical techniques and instruments in the field of educational research
- A presentation of core educational concepts
- An overview of a testing and evaluation method
- A snapshot of a hot or emerging topic or policy change
- An in-depth case study
- A literature review
- A report/review study of a survey
- An elaborated thesis

Both solicited and unsolicited manuscripts are considered for publication in the SpringerBriefs in Education series. Potential authors are warmly invited to complete and submit the Briefs Author Proposal form. All projects will be submitted to editorial review by editorial advisors.

SpringerBriefs are characterized by expedited production schedules with the aim for publication 8 to 12 weeks after acceptance and fast, global electronic dissemination through our online platform SpringerLink. The standard concise author contracts guarantee that:

- an individual ISBN is assigned to each manuscript
- each manuscript is copyrighted in the name of the author
- the author retains the right to post the pre-publication version on his/her website or that of his/her institution

More information about this series at http://www.springer.com/series/8914

Dominic Orr · Maren Luebcke ·
J. Philipp Schmidt · Markus Ebner ·
Klaus Wannemacher · Martin Ebner ·
Dieter Dohmen

Higher Education Landscape 2030

A Trend Analysis Based on the AHEAD
International Horizon Scanning

GEFÖRDERT VOM

Bundesministerium
für Bildung
und Forschung

Dominic Orr (ID)
FiBS Research Institute for the Economics
of Education and Social Affairs
Berlin, Germany

Maren Luebcke
HIS Institute for Higher Education
Development (HIS-HE)
Hannover, Germany

J. Philipp Schmidt
Massachusetts Institute of Technology
Cambridge, MA, USA

Markus Ebner (ID)
Graz University of Technology
Graz, Austria

Klaus Wannemacher (ID)
HIS Institute for Higher Education
Development (HIS-HE)
Hannover, Germany

Martin Ebner (ID)
Graz University of Technology
Graz, Austria

Dieter Dohmen
FiBS Research Institute for the Economics
of Education and Social Affairs
Berlin, Germany

ISSN 2211-1921   ISSN 2211-193X   (electronic)
SpringerBriefs in Education
ISBN 978-3-030-44896-7   ISBN 978-3-030-44897-4   (eBook)
https://doi.org/10.1007/978-3-030-44897-4

Institut für
Hochschulentwicklung

**Forschungsinstitut für
Bildungs- und Sozialökonomie**

Research Institute for the Economics
of Education and Social Affairs

Sponsored by the Federal Ministry of Education and Research

The original version of the book was revised: The corresponding author has been changed. The correction to the book is available at https://doi.org/10.1007/978-3-030-44897-4_5

About This Book

Between February 2018 and January 2019, a systematic analysis of current trends and requirements in the areas of knowledge and competence was carried out within the project "(A) Higher Education Digital (AHEAD)—International Horizon Scanning/Trend Analysis on Digital Higher Education." One aim of this project was to examine the latest developments in learning theory, didactics, and digital-education technology against the background of (increasingly) digitized higher education. The analysis formed the basis for a horizon scanning of higher education in 2030, designed to develop future scenarios that would meet future higher education demands by taking advantage of social and digital innovations.

This study was conducted on behalf of the German Federal Ministry of Education and Research (BMBF) by the FiBS Research Institute for the Economics of Education and Social Affairs together with the HIS Institute for Higher Education Development e.V. (HIS-HE).

The AHEAD study was commissioned to look into the future and reveal what the higher education landscape could look like in 2030. The study takes account of technological developments in society, without seeing them as the sole force driving future higher education. Rather, it assumes that higher education will change by 2030 as a result of developments in the following areas:

- Knowledge and competence requirements from industry and social changes, in an increasingly digitalized world;
- New developments in didactics, reflecting current discussions in the field of didactics and learning theory;
- Digital technologies and new ways of using these technologies, which are likely to create new forms of learning and environments for learning.

This study was conducted in two phases. First, preliminary studies were carried out to investigate the three areas mentioned above, using literature evaluations, surveys, interviews, and subsequent discussions with the AHEAD International Advisory Board.

A comparative literature analysis at the beginning of the study clearly revealed thematic focal points by discipline; the findings are summarized in the following three core statements, which are central to the research approach adopted here:

– The literature shows that the economic view of the future of higher education is clearly focused on students, in the context of the labor market and labor-market requirements.
– The educational science perspective, on the other hand, emphasizes the role of learning and the skills and competences that students will need to succeed in the labor market.
– Technology and digitization are central topics only in the field of computer science.

A comprehensive view of higher education in 2030 must merge all of these perspectives into one picture of the future.

An examination of other predictive studies of higher education shows that many future scenarios focus on institutions of higher education and examine the question of what such institutions could look like in 2030. However, this question depends not only on demand, but also on the freedom to shape and reform higher education, which is determined by governance regulations, including laws, financing methods, and quality assurance.

The AHEAD study has therefore adopted a different perspective. The project team, in cooperation with the Advisory Board, and following discussions with many experts and stakeholders, decided to put learners at the center of the concept—because higher education exists to support learners. The demands of the labor market and society have an impact on learners, who remain central to good didactic concepts. Digital technologies allow more flexible learning, as well as opportunities to learn in very different spaces, blurring the boundary between physical and virtual presence.

In the second phase of the project, four learning pathways were developed to provide a view of higher education in 2030. These learning pathways and their elaboration were based on interviews with experts and initiators of innovative learning opportunities, group discussions, and an international survey conducted by the team during the project. In addition, innovative use cases were researched to illustrate these learning paths. The learning pathways are briefly described below (named after toys for ease of recall):

– *"Tamagotchi:"* Here, as at present, the study program offers basic, comprehensive preparation for subsequent employment, with the university functioning as a closed ecosystem that supports and guides students as they pursue a course of study. This model is particularly well-suited to people who go (almost) directly from school to university or college.
– *"Jenga:"* In this model, the "first-degree" program offers a solid foundation of knowledge and competences, and can take the form of a shortened study program. The curriculum builds on this foundation and is constantly expanded by the learner (student) through new learning blocks. These additional blocks are made available by various training providers.

- *"Lego:"* The course of study is no longer completed as a compact unit at a university or college, but consists of individually combined modules of different sizes from different training providers. The learners themselves decide which learning phases or units they want to complete. In addition to providing the learning units, the university is responsible for recognizing completed learning phases by providing formal certificates or documentation.
- *"Transformer:"* The students in this model do not transfer directly to higher education as school-leavers, but have already acquired their own professional identities and life experiences. They attend university or college later in life integrating their life experience into their studies. They need a flexible course of study that alternates between didactic control by teachers and advisors, and their own self-determination.

This vision of a higher education landscape that emanates from the learner has been shown to foster open discussion. As a result of this change in perspective, questions about institutional support, governance, and quality assurance, as well as issues involving institutional financing for restructuring and infrastructure (which would otherwise have a major impact on any debate about the future form of higher education or higher education institutions) move into second place. Although the suggested learning pathways will have a substantial impact on the organization and activities of universities and colleges, as well as on higher education policy and governance, the present study will not investigate this topic further.

The use cases described in this study show how technology can be fully embedded into educational initiatives. The practical examples showcase a new strategic approach that is not merely additive but highlights daring reform efforts, avoiding the less promising approach of placing new technology in old structures. Innovation is not simply based on technology but on the use of new technologies to achieve (higher) education goals more fully and effectively for all.

The FiBS Research Institute for the Economics of Education and Social Affairs

The FiBS Research Institute for the Economics of Education and Social Affairs (Forschungsinstitut für Bildungs- und Sozialökonomie) is an independent institution that carries out application-oriented research and consulting on lifelong learning, from early childhood education to continuing education; it is based in Berlin and interfaces with the labor market, innovation, digitization, social issues, and demographic development. The institute is active in Germany, Europe, and worldwide; its mission statement is "Enhancing Lifelong Learning for All."

FiBS was founded in 1993 by its owner and director, Dr. Dieter Dohmen, as interdisciplinary research and consulting institution and think tank, with a focus on science-based policy advice. For more than 15 years, a key area of focus has been the impact of digitization on education, learning, and the labor market. In addition to the present study, which investigates the implications of digitization on universities, particularly in relation to vocational education and training (with a focus on developing countries), we have developed market potentials and business models for the higher education sector at an early stage. Currently, we are also working to integrate this topic into curricula.

The HIS Institute for Higher Education Development (HIS-HE)

The HIS Institute for Higher Education Development (HIS-Institut für Hochschulentwicklung e. V., HIS-HE) is dedicated to the promotion of science, research, and teaching. This research-based, independent competence center specializes in consulting and know-how transfer on topics that relate to university development and the organization of research and teaching. The federal states of the Federal Republic of Germany are members of the HIS Institute for Higher Education Development.

   With the HIS Institute for Higher Education Development, the German Länder maintain an institution whose profile enables the development of basic principles for the construction, use, and organization of universities, research, and educational institutions; it also provides planning assistance and policy advice on questions of strategy, management, organization, and process design, as well as technical and structural equipment.

Contents

About the Authors

Dr. Dominic Orr holds a Ph.D. in Comparative Educational Science from the Technical University of Dresden and is a Professor of Educational Management at the University of Nova Gorica. From 2015 to early 2019, he was the project manager and senior researcher at FiBS Research Institute for the Economics of Education and Social Affairs and is currently a senior researcher at Kiron Open Higher Education. He has also worked on the relationship between research, policy, and practice in many international contexts, including as a consultant for the OECD, UNESCO, and the World Bank. In addition to leading this AHEAD project, he is a member of the MIRVA project, which aims to make the recognition of skills and competencies through digital badge technologies visible and valuable.

Dr. Maren Luebcke is a research associate in the Department of University Management at the HIS Institute for Higher Education Development (HIS-HE) in Hanover. Her consulting and research focus at HIS-HE is the digitization of research and teaching at universities. She holds a Ph.D. in Communication and Internet Sociology and a Master of Higher Education. She has worked in various international research projects on e-learning and e-democracy and is the author of various publications in this field.

J. Philipp Schmidt is Director of Learning Innovation at MIT Media Lab where he leads, teaches, and develops ML Learning initiative. He is also a co-founder and board member of Peer 2 Peer University (P2PU), a nonprofit organization that provides access to higher education through public libraries.

Markus Ebner is a junior researcher in the Organizational Unit Teaching and Learning Technologies at the Graz University of Technology. His doctoral thesis deals with the areas of e-learning, mobile learning, technology-enhanced learning, and open educational resources. He focuses on learning analytics in the primary and secondary school environment and on educational informatics.

Dr. Klaus Wannemacher is a senior consultant and project manager in the University Management Division of the HIS Institute for Higher Education Development (HIS-HE). As an organizational consultant, he supports universities, nonuniversity research institutions, and ministries with consulting services and research projects with a focus on the digital transformation at universities in research, teaching, and administration. In 2016, the Society for Media in Science (GMW) appointed him as a Fellow. In 2017, the German Rectors' Conference nominated him for participation in the "Digital Information" initiative of the Alliance of German Science Organisations.

Priv.-Doz. Dr. Martin Ebner is the head of the Department of Teaching and Learning Technologies at the Graz University of Technology, where he is responsible for all e-learning issues. Furthermore, he researches and teaches as a habilitated media information scientist (specialist field: educational informatics) at the Institute for Interactive Systems and Data Science around technology-supported learning. His main focuses are seamless learning, learning analytics, open educational resources, maker education, and informatics basic education. He blogs at http://elearningblog. tugraz.at and further details can be found at http://www. martinebner.at

Dr. Dieter Dohmen is the founder, owner, and Director of the FiBS Research Institute for Educational and Social Economics and works as a scientist and consultant, currently in Germany as well as in various other European and non-European countries. He is the Scientific Director of all projects. After his studies in sports and social sciences at the German Sport University Cologne and the University of Cologne, he obtained a diploma in economics and social sciences at the University of Cologne and a doctorate at the Technical University Berlin.

List of Figures

List of Tables

Chapter 1
A University Landscape for the Digital World

Abstract As the digital transformation clearly highlights the role of universities and institutes of higher education in shaping a higher education system that is more open and provides education to everyone who can benefit from it, this study seeks to analyze, in more detail, what developments are having an impact on higher education and develops future scenarios for education in 2030. The UK study *Solving future skills challenges* implies that the linear model of education–employment–career will no longer be sufficient in the future, requiring new combinations of skills, experience, and collaboration from educators and employers. This UK study serves as a starting point for the AHEAD trend analysis for a higher education landscape in 2030. Five premises ranging from "No naive innovation view" to "Realistic approach," and "Diversity in higher education" provide the basis for a search for concepts for the higher education of the future.

In the future, universities and institutes of higher education will play an even more central role in managing and shaping the digital transformation.

Higher education fulfills several objectives for society. In the areas of research and teaching, it primarily creates an educational space to prepare for the future. It prepares students for their further personal and professional development, which will be subject to considerable dynamics. It also provides a space for reflexive thinking about what it means to be a citizen of the globalized, digitized world, ultimately offering students opportunities to further develop their character and attitudes.

In addition, the higher education system will need to be more open in the future, providing access to quality education to everyone who can benefit from it.[1] This study addresses the relationship between higher education and initial and continuing vocational education and training, which are still strongly separated in most worldwide education systems (and particularly in Germany).

---

[1] Among OECD countries and countries in the European Higher Education Area, higher education continues to be socially selective (Blossfeld et al., 2017; European Commission/EACEA/Eurydice, 2018).

© FiBS - Forschungsinstitut für Bildungs- und Sozialökonomie, and HIS-Institut für Hochschulentwicklung e.V. (HIS-HE) 2020
D. Orr et al., *Higher Education Landscape 2030*,
SpringerBriefs in Education, https://doi.org/10.1007/978-3-030-44897-4_1

The potential of digitization for universities lies not only in the function it can add through e-learning but also in its integrative force, which can improve higher education as a whole, as the 2018 position paper, "Bologna Digital," makes clear (Gibb, Hofer, & Klofsten, 2018; Orr, van der Hijden, Rampelt, Röwert, & Suter, 2018a, 2018b). The present study incorporates this idea.

Digitization will lead to changes in the higher education landscape; indications of such changes are presented here. This study does not assume that the university landscape as a whole will be a victim of destructive innovation ("disruption"). The high expectations associated with innovations developed in the Silicon Valley environment (keyword: MOOCs) have not yet revolutionized higher education. Instead, universities have adopted these innovations and integrated them into existing degree programs (Jansen & Konings, 2017; Reich & Ruipérez-Valiente, 2019). However, digital developments can also help universities redefine and better fulfill their role. The emergence of innovative new models and organizations will enrich the higher education landscape. Future progress is not just a matter of retrofitting longstanding higher education approaches (Kelly & Hess, 2013), but also of extending them to foster sustainable changes.

What is meant by "Digitization" as a Process?

According to the Oxford English Dictionary, digitization is the conversion of a text, image, or sound into a digital form that can be processed by a computer. This material process in itself has little influence. To achieve a significant impact, digitization must be integrated into a far-reaching process—and a corresponding ecosystem—that uses digital materials for digital transformation (in short: digitalization) (Brennen & Kreiss, 2016). The Internet and digital networks are means to connect different types of information, to generate new data flows, and to structure communication channels for improved interaction between people and processes. The new information nodes and networks enable a new form of process organization (Castells, 2010; Cerwal, 2017). The application of new digital technologies is therefore not only a question of what technology can do but also how it interacts with other established practices and individual and organizational routines. The particular challenge of the twenty-first century is to ensure that all sectors benefit from the increasing digital transformation of society.

The aim of this study is to analyze in more detail the developments that are having a major impact on the environment of higher education, and to develop scenarios for higher education in 2030 on this basis. The present study thus meets a central demand of the position paper by Baumgartner (2018) on the future role of higher education: "We need more creative scenarios with which we can think about the future of social developments and their possible consequences for our institutions (such as universities)."

The organization that represents universities in the UK has recently carried out a study of higher education requirements in a digital, networked world (Universities UK, 2018). The conclusion of this study provides a suitable starting point for the AHEAD study:

> The linear model of education–employment–career will no longer be sufficient. The pace of change is accelerating, necessitating more flexible partnerships, quicker responses, different modes of delivery and new combinations of skills and experience. Educators and employers need to collaborate more closely, and develop new and innovative partnerships and flexible learning approaches. (ibid.)

Thus, concepts are sought for the higher education of the future, which must become stronger and stronger, while building on the current structure of higher education. Such concepts could have an evolutionary and transformative effect on today's higher education system.

This search is based on the following five premises:

- **No naive innovation view**: It can be assumed that some parts of the (institutionalized) system will resemble the current one, while innovations will emerge both within this system and through new organizations.
- **Transfer and renewal through digitization**: Digitization is expected to have an impact on many areas of higher education provision and beyond. In addition, new forms of higher education will become increasingly sustainable and scalable.
- **Realistic**: The scenarios should, where possible, have points of contact with current systems of higher education, allowing their potential, including the tensions inherent in the models, to be demonstrated on the basis of exemplary developments. The year 2030 has been chosen as a future endpoint to ensure that innovations are linked to the current situation and the perspective does not become too speculative.
- **The perspective of the learner**: The learner's path through the educational system is the focus of this investigation. The educational provisions offered by universities depend on learner requirements.
- **Diversity in higher education**: In contrast to other future-oriented studies, this paper does not assume that there will be *one* model of higher education in the future. Instead, we assume that the higher education landscape will continue to become more diversified and that alternative learning and higher education paths will develop in response to various challenges and ultimately coexist. For this reason, the study refers to "higher education" in general, and not simply to institutes of higher education.

Chapter 2
From Lines of Development to Scenarios

Abstract After examining the current developments in the field of knowledge and competence requirements, university teaching and technology, and their effects on a digital society through various background studies, this chapter focuses on modeling and developing different scenarios and discussions with regard to technology and social developments. Different economic and social requirements as well as new forms of didactics and learning environments will lead to necessary changes in higher education. It should provide a link between continuing and higher education by identifying new ways of recognizing skills acquired informally. Strong support most notably for new students, should combine performing, developing, and explorative teaching and learning situations. Meanwhile, it will be essential for the didactics of the future to be sensitive to the needs of learners and offer individualized support for student-learning paths, making education independent of time and place. Finally, selected approaches to developing future scenarios in higher education focusing on institutions and governance issues, technology, and social developments are discussed in more detail.

The study assumes that higher education will change by 2030 as a result of developments in the following areas:

- Knowledge and competence requirements emerging from the economy, as well as social changes in an increasingly digitalized world;
- New developments in didactics, arising from didactic discussions of the subject;
- Digital technologies and new uses of technology that enable new forms of learning and learning environments.

As a first step, this study used methods of systematic analysis, based on the literature review, data analysis, interviews, and expert discussions, to identify likely potential changes in the future higher education landscape. To scan the higher education horizon (Amanatidou et al., 2012), these analyses have been condensed into future scenarios in the second step; they have been validated and further developed

© FiBS - Forschungsinstitut für Bildungs- und Sozialökonomie, and HIS-Institut
für Hochschulentwicklung e.V. (HIS-HE) 2020
D. Orr et al., *Higher Education Landscape 2030*,
SpringerBriefs in Education, https://doi.org/10.1007/978-3-030-44897-4_2

through a broad discussion with experts from the university sector, politics, and students. In addition, innovative practical examples have been sought from all parts of the world and incorporated into the developing scenario, as possible future models.

Detailed information on all of these areas can be found in the appendix.[1] The following section presents the most important results of the investigation, which have significantly influenced the scenario-development process.

2.1 Background Studies

2.1.1 A Literature Analysis and the Future of Higher Education

The Big Data approach was initially used to carry out a literature and citation analysis, with specialist literature[2] identified via the Web of Science database. The central search terms were as follows: higher education/universit[y/ies], futur[e], digital, work, competenc[y/ies], and labo[u]r [market/force]. A total of 15,249 predominantly English-language articles, published during the last 40 years, were included in the analysis (83% were published during the last ten years).

This data set was analyzed thematically to determine the importance of certain topics in the literature. Ten thematic terms were used for the analysis; these were searched for in titles, abstracts, and keywords. The thematic terms covered the following areas: learning; knowledge; skills (competency, skills, learning); teaching; students; the labor market; work; technology (technology, digital); other aspects of digitization (digital divide, data security); and higher education. A meta-analysis of the main topics by discipline provides the first glimpse into discussions about the future of universities. This analysis, however, has focused on selections in which the words "*future*" and "*university*" appear together ($n = 8359$). Figure 2.1 compares the priorities of the educational sciences, psychology, business studies, and computer science.[3]

This comparative analysis clearly shows the thematic focus of the contributions by discipline; the findings can be summarized in the following three core statements:

1. The economic view of the future of universities is clearly focused on students, within the context of the labor market and labor market requirements.

---

[1] The appendix is only available in German.

[2] This database holds and provides an index of published literature (in particular, articles from scientific journals) in a wide range of disciplines, including medicine, the natural sciences, humanities, the social sciences, and economics.

[3] Individual contributions can also be assigned to several disciplines.

Fig. 2.1 Frequency of named keywords in the body of literature studied (The terms "digital divide" and "data security" do not appear in all of the illustrations because they occurred so rarely). *Source* Own illustration

Literature from the field of computer sciences (n=441)

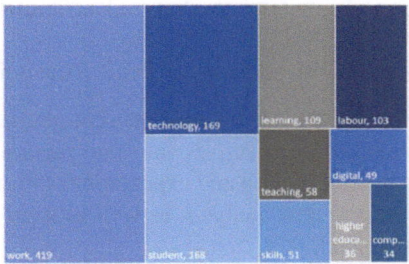

Literature from the field of education sciences (n=2686)

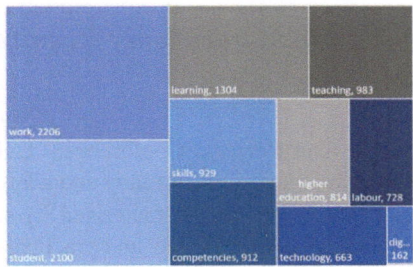

Literature from the field of psychology (n=607)

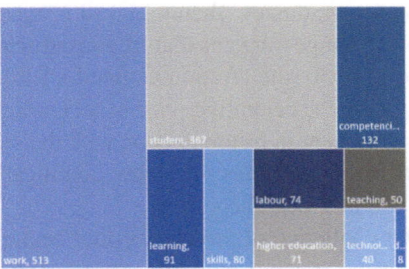

Literature from the field of business studies (n=629)

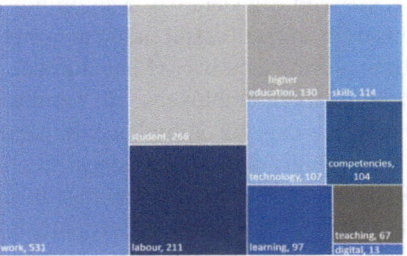

2. By contrast, the educational science perspective emphasizes the role of learning and the skills and competences that students must acquire to succeed in the labor market.
3. Technology and digitization are thematic focal points for computer science only.

This insight leads to the conclusion that a comprehensive view of higher education in 2030 must unite all perspectives into one picture of the future. The following sections present the findings on and expectations of future higher education obtained from the literature and data analysis, as well as from expert interviews on the three perspectives mentioned.

2.1.2 Knowledge and Competence Requirements of a Digital Society

According to the German Rectors' Conference, "Universities are the 'engines' of economic and social innovation in Germany and a key sector for the road to 'Industry 4.0'" (HRK, 2018). They are characterized by the promotion of professional development, the transfer of knowledge, and practical education. Accordingly, it is a priority for higher education to prepare for central trends and movements in society, but also to shape such developments. It is not enough to focus solely on the new generation of university graduates. Technological progress in a digital world—coupled with demographic change—means that **higher education** must finally be **opened to all**. With regard to 2030, the "Action Council on Education" (Aktionsrat Bildung) writes: "In view of the accelerating pace of technological progress, however, it will be less and less sufficient in future to cope with the structural change in occupations through the arrival of graduates with new qualifications" (Blossfeld et al., 2017). Older workers will also need new skills.

The particular challenge of the twenty-first century is to ensure that all parts of society benefit from the increasing integration of digitization into society. Discussions about future requirements of the labor market, due to the effects of automation, artificial intelligence, and Big Data-based algorithms, point to massive changes. It is expected that this dynamic will result in the majority of graduates **changing career paths several times** during their lives (Manyika et al., 2017; OECD, 2017a). In many sectors of the labor market, employees will require retraining and new learning to reposition themselves as capable of implementing the technologically improved processes that will increasingly define their workplaces. It is the task of business, interest groups, and politicians to promote and facilitate this process of change.

Many recent studies of labor market developments have addressed the polarization expected as a result of increasing digitization. The trend is toward tasks that require more advanced professional skills, coupled with social, and emotional skills as the study of selected OECD countries has shown (Nedelkoska & Quintini, 2018). In addition, the labor market is eroding. Professions that require mid-level qualifications (i.e., high-level technical training but no academic degree) and involve moderately difficult routine tasks, appear to be declining. Such professions are costly enough to justify investing in their replacement but routine enough to be susceptible to replacement by automation (OECD, 2016; Zenhäusern & Vaterlaus, 2017).

However, another OECD analysis has shown that, in most sectors of the economy, the decline in employment at the intermediate-qualification level is fully offset by growth at the high-qualification level (OECD, 2017b). To date, the two sectors that have experienced the greatest changes in this direction are the paper and publishing industry and the financial and insurance sectors. In the wholesale and retail trade and hotel and restaurant sectors, employment by skill level has declined, contrary to the general trend (i.e., jobs are being cut in these sectors). Even when such transformations do not lead to job losses, an analysis of job markets in Germany and Austria has shown that wages for employees unable to make this change are declining (Südekum, 2018).

Where these analyses are broad in scope, they conceal differences between occupations that require an intermediate level of skill. An analysis based on the US data has shown the same decline in medium-skilled jobs, with weak growth in some sectors. Holzer has identified "new medium-sized jobs" that are currently being created in the labor market (Holzer, 2015). The professions involved include specialized health technicians (e.g., phlebotomists, X-ray technicians), paralegals, security services, cooks, managers of food and beverage companies, retail managers, and field representatives. In contrast to the "old middle," most of these modern workplaces expect their employees to carry out relatively complex technical, administrative, or communicative tasks. An expanding and differentiating working population needs more opportunities to engage in higher education at different phases of life; learners from this group also have very different educational biographies.

The central role of economic institutions is to find new forms of organization, production, and supply processes to ensure their economic survival and success. As **learning also takes place within business enterprises**, it makes sense to integrate learning experiences more effectively through exchanges between companies and universities.

It is the responsibility of the education system **to educate and train future and current workers, ensuring that they acquire appropriate knowledge and skills**. The education system must ensure that current workers can benefit from new developments, while also enabling new generations of entrepreneurs to become reflective and innovative and to create new businesses that operate sustainably in a global world.

Workers must be resilient enough to cope with change; they must be able to reposition themselves throughout their careers. They must also be creative enough to solve problems and develop new ideas for future progress. Many people are expected to work in jobs that do not exist today. A work report proposed 21 such jobs, including Human–Machine–Teaming Managers, Big Data Detectives, AI-based Personal Health Technicians, Digital Tailors, and Personal Data Brokers (Pring, Brown, Davis, Bahl, & Cook, 2017). Although such jobs are unlikely to represent a large section of the future labor market in 2030, all employees will need to be tech-savvy. A central aspect of many workplaces will revolve around enabling people (with different backgrounds and specializations) and machines to work together in teams to exploit the possibilities of personal data securely while protecting personal identity. What is certain, therefore, is that the **mix of standardized knowledge, new knowledge, and transversal skills** in all training programs will have to be reviewed regularly in the future (OECD, 2018b; Universities UK, 2018).

The demand for university graduates in the labor market, both in terms of employment levels and relative wage premiums (European Commission/EACEA/Eurydice, 2018), indicates that university graduates are already acquiring some of these competences through their studies or as students. However, this is not the whole truth. A European survey of new recruits found that graduates were much less likely to feel underqualified in their new jobs (i.e., that their current skills were below their job demands in self-assessments) than were employees whose formal education was below university level (CEDEFOP, 2018). Nevertheless, the same study also showed that more than a fifth of all graduates felt poorly prepared for their new jobs.

As shown in Fig. 2.2, graduates were most likely to feel underqualified in the fields of engineering, medicine, and agriculture. The authors of the present study have assumed that this finding reflects (among other things) a constantly changing qualification context, due to the continuing development of new technologies, working methods, and techniques (CEDEFOP, 2018). Another study, based on the same dataset, has argued that the lack of standard knowledge in these specific areas is a less significant issue than deficits in soft skills, such as patient-communication skills and teamwork preparation (Livanos & Nunez, 2015). These deficits in the preparation and support of medicine are already widely discussed in Germany (Kuhn, Jungmann, Deutsch, Drees, & Rommens, 2018).

These data initially reflect the transition from education to working life. In an innovative environment, such learning curves are likely to be repeated, as jobs are reorganized and practices changed to make the best use of digital opportunities over

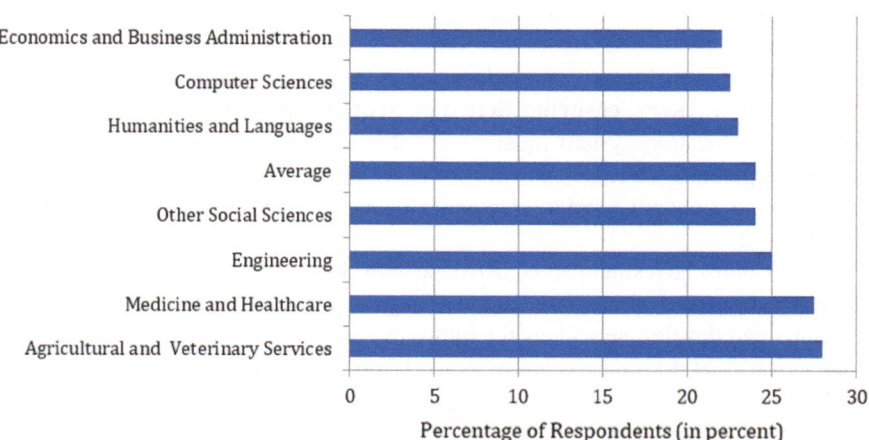

Fig. 2.2 Perception of being unqualified among graduates recruited by subject area (selected areas), share 2014 (EU-28). *Source* Cedefop European skills and job survey (ESJS)

the course of a career (Bessen, 2015). As **the question of the optimal knowledge and competence profile for employees** continues to arise and be debated, new learning options seem necessary.

Conclusion: Requirements for Higher Education in 2030

Higher education can contribute to meeting the challenges posed by changes in the labor market through the following measures:

- All higher education programs should review their learning objectives to ensure that they explicitly address learning that combines disciplinary knowledge, basic skills, transversal skills, and digital skills.
- As multiple skills will need to be combined and applied simultaneously in an (often international) teamwork environment, authentic learning that establishes a strong link to future workplaces will become an increasingly important didactic tool.
- As changes in the labor market increase, employees will require more frequent learning processes and experiences. To meet this need, opportunities to begin and leave degree programs should be made more flexible (e.g., through modules and credits). Learning opportunities should be provided in ways that allow people to complete aspects of learning alongside their careers.
- In the future, employees without a university degree will tend to work in occupations in which a high degree of automation can be expected. Their skill profiles are more likely to be deficient in basic, transversal, and digital skills; they are also less likely to receive further training over the course of their careers. Higher education providers can help to reintegrate such employees into formal education.
- Since informal learning (at least) takes place continuously throughout most people's lives, one way to activate further learning paths is to identify new ways of recognizing skills learned informally, as an aspect of formal learning paths, both during and potentially through higher education. Universities could establish themselves as important actors by providing accreditation and learning support to the whole population. To achieve a highly responsive higher education sector, it will be essential to strengthen the cooperation between continuing and higher education, as the current structure lacks clear linear pathways from higher education to career development. Supplements from continuing education alone are unlikely to resolve this challenge in the future.

2.1.3 University Didactics-Related Challenges for a Digital Society

This section investigates the university from an internal perspective, identifying the trends expected to shape university didactics in the year 2030. The term "didactics" denotes the relationship between content (What is to be taught?), activation/motivation (How do learners succeed in being motivated to learn?), and support (How are learners accompanied in learning?) (Reinmann, 2015).[4] For the period up to 2030, didactics are likely to focus on activating learners, rather than the range of courses on offer. Although this so-called "shift from teaching to learning" is not new (Barr & Tagg, 1995; Cedefop, 2009), it is likely to remain a dominant paradigm in the context of digitally supported learning arrangements that offer effective learning scenarios to heterogeneous groups of learners.

An analysis of the relevant educational and pedagogical literature, carried out within this study, confirms that the question of learning is prominent in higher education.[5] The topic includes student learning, student engagement, and students' capacity for self-efficacy and self-regulation. Even the assessment of learning outcomes is offered to students as individuals or in their role as "peers." The teachers and teaching disappear almost completely behind them.

The textual evaluation of relevant articles shows that a wide range of terms is associated with the topic "learning," corresponding to the new didactic triangle between active learning, technology, and network structures (see Fig. 2.3). New technologies, coupled with high user competence and acceptance and the network effects of social platforms, can support a more inductive and collaborative form of learning.

Expert surveys and interviews carried out during the investigation of this complex of topics also reflect the diversity of future forms of learning. From the expert point of view, the question of how learning spaces can be structured, sometimes collaboratively and sometimes autonomously, will be relevant at least until 2030 (Schön, Ebner, & Schön, 2016).

The question of whether digitally supported methods should be used for learning is suppressed. Instead, a "fusion" of forms of learning can be observed, carried out more frequently on-campus and online. This structure requires **flexibility in the roles of teachers and students** and in the configuration of their interrelationships and learning content (Miyazoe & Anderson, 2013; Moore, 1993) (see Table 2.1). This poses a significant challenge for the future.

---

[4]During an early phase of project development, the authors of the study were advised on university didactics-related challenges by Sandra Hofhues, whose suggestions were incorporated into this chapter and the in-depth report "A3 University Teaching Challenges within a Digital Society" (see Annex 6.1.3). The authors thank Sandra Hofhues for her support.

[5]Articles published in the following journals in 2017–2018 were evaluated ($n = 509$): *Internet and Higher Education, Research in Higher Education, Journal of Higher Education, Studies in Higher Education, Review of Higher Education, Community College Review, Assessment and Evaluation in Higher Education, Active Learning in Higher Education, Higher Education Research and Development, Journal of Computing in Higher Education, and Perspectives: Policy and Practice in Higher Education.*

Fig. 2.3 Literature analysis—the evaluation of frequencies in the category "learning." *Source* Own illustration

Table 2.1 Various learning arrangements

Learning arrangement	Presenting	Moderating	Exploring
The teaching procedure is …	teacher-led, deductive	teacher-led, inductive	learner-led, inductive
The role of teachers is …	leading, guiding	developing, guiding	stimulating, advising
The role of the learner is …	receiving comprehensively	participating, thinking, instructing, working	working independently
The learning content …	is provided by teachers and received by learners	is determined by learners and teachers together and worked on by learners under guidance	is worked on by learners independently

Source Schön et al. (2016)

The expert survey particularly emphasized the need to reorient didactics, in the context of digitization. The standard model of classroom teaching needs further development. Presence learning will be combined with web-based learning processes. In addition, **new institutional formats for didactic self-reflection** and the development of teaching and learning cultures will be needed to keep pace with increasing processes of change. Bottom-up developments, resulting from the active practice of teachers and learners, must be embraced.

By contrast, important trend reports on this topic highlight the qualitative changes that are influencing the demand for study programs. Demand will increase for life-long learning courses, online and blended-learning courses, credential unbundling, and courses that add the greatest value to professional careers. These demands will ultimately lead to new types of offers being made in the field of higher education.

Sensitivity and openness in higher education will be necessary, especially in relation to learning content. Research shows that the **development of "studyability"** is a long-term process that usually starts in school but continues through the initial phase of education. In Germany, as in other countries, most universities have introduced support and bridge courses to meet this demand. The expert interviews emphasized the central importance of such support measures, which can respond to the differing needs of learners. In particular, attention must be paid to the future development and support of student-learning empowerment, i.e., students' competence at self-regulated learning, which is central to both "working" and "explorative" learning arrangements. As students from underrepresented groups are often uncertain about their choice of field (Hauschildt, Vögtle, & Gwosć, 2018), too much flexibility in educational design could exacerbate this uncertainty.

Digitization may offer some solutions. It has been shown that digital **bridge and support programs** can help to reduce student concerns by offering better study orientation (Bidarra & Rusman, 2017; Ubachs, Konings, & Brown, 2017). According-ing to the experts, learning processes in higher education are individualized; more effective learning is achieved through learning analytics—for example, when the data generated in learning-management systems are evaluated and used to optimize learning processes. This also means that the higher education system must increasingly rely on the enhanced competence of teaching staff, who must understand how this information can be used to promote learning.

Openness in higher education is needed to provide learning plans, objectives, and curricula. In addition to enabling students to acquire general skills (including soft skills and "learning to learn"), higher education teaches specific bodies of knowledge and skills required for particular fields of work or specializations (e.g., engineering or law); these build the foundation for workplace effectiveness. To identify and transmit such knowledge and skills, stakeholders must reach a consensus on the abilities needed in particular areas. In an era of digitization, this consensus will be subject to constant review (Eckert et al., 2018). Analogous to "Industry 4.0" (see Sect. 2.1.2), higher education needs a "Curriculum 4.0".

> As a Curriculum 4.0, we understand a curriculum that takes up the process of digital trans-formation in a targeted manner, both in terms of content and at the level of the skills and competences to be taught. (…) [We] view digital change in the context of curriculum devel-opment holistically as a technical, didactic, and content-related challenge. (Michel et al., 2018)

Effective and individualized university didactics must be based on educational research, which examines and improves learning and educational processes and investigates the impact of learning arrangements. Both the literature and expert discussions revealed deficits in this area that must be resolved by 2030 if higher education is to become more effective and inclusive. In addition, the educational mandate must be increasingly reflected in society.

Michael Feldstein, a well-known expert from the American educational technology sector, published a pointed presentation on this situation at the beginning of 2019. In his view, new technological developments will only improve learning if educational research can establish a basic consensus on the central dimensions of the learning system:

> This is not something that could be 'overhauled' by the magic of machine learning. (…) We investigate complex processes that we largely cannot see. When we develop tools that give us visibility, we often lack the theoretical foundation (…) to understand what we see. With many things we learn, we do not yet know how to apply them, and much of what we can apply is separate from our still blurred picture of how learning works. (Feldstein, 2019)

Conclusion: Requirements for Higher Education 2030

The further development of higher education didactics will play a central role in creating effective and inclusive higher education for all. The following factors are particularly important:

- The provision of flexible higher education depends on didactics that are sensitive to the needs of learners and open to the needs of society and the labor market.
- Higher education is based on the didactic triangle between active learning, technology, and network structures; this triangle mediates, appropriates, and explores learning materials. Digitized solutions can support learning processes and interactions between learners.
- Up-to-date didactics for higher education in 2030 will include new institutional formats for didactic self-reflection; they will increasingly incorporate bottom-up developments from teaching and learning practice.
- Most learners need strong support, at least at the beginning of their study careers. This is particularly true for learners who finished school many years earlier. Learning arrangements should, therefore, combine performing, developing, and explorative teaching and learning situations that offer more or less support to learners, depending on their career and educational biographies. Digital and attendance phases are both needed, intertwined throughout the learning strategy or curriculum.
- During the learning phase, an open system of higher education will observe and react to developments outside the university or formal learning setting. One particular challenge will be to find didactic methods that bring structure and control to this open system, creating a learning path that remains transparent to students and teachers alike. Learning analytics and other methods of observing learning are recommended.

- Research on universities and education will be needed to underpin, critically question, and improve these processes.

2.1.4   Technological Conditions and Opportunities for Higher Education in a Digital Society

In its recommendations on the differentiation of universities in 2010, the Council of Science and Humanities emphasized the importance of universities as physical places and studies as social practices. Digitization was seen as a marginal topic, related to e-learning (Wissenschaftsrat, 2010). In the future, the **contrast between physical and virtual space will become less and less important**—in fact, the two spaces will "merge" (Schön et al., 2016) (see Fig. 2.4).

In 2030, higher education will be characterized by digital opportunities, digital technologies, and infrastructures, as well as support structures. To better understand these opportunities and challenges, two groups of experts were interviewed on the basis of these guidelines: The first group was composed of technical experts from "classical" universities in Germany, Austria, and Switzerland (11 interviews). The results of these interviews are summarized in the section, "Views from the mainstream higher education sector." The second group was composed of program leaders of innovative initiatives in or adjacent to higher education (11 interviews in six countries); these are discussed in the section, "Operational and strategic benefits of technology in higher education."

2.1.4.1   View from the Mainstream University Sector

Most experts agreed that video-based courses could be offered in supplementary or exclusively online formats. Through control questions and tracking, each individual's learning progress can be monitored and adapted to his or her needs, using

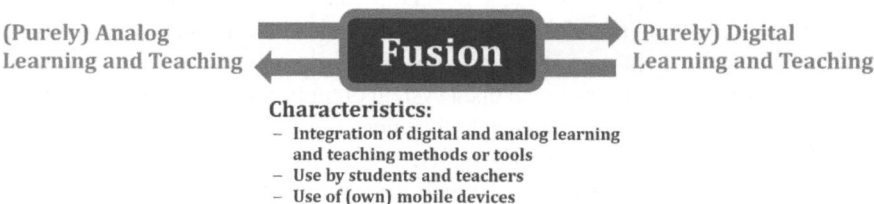

Fig. 2.4 New learning spaces that integrate analogue and digital approaches. *Source* Schön et al. (2016)

learning analytics. The availability of a range of online channels and materials makes it possible to reach students outside traditional teaching units. This enables learning, independent of location and time. Individual study (of specialist or less popular subjects) could become the norm.

Digitally supported scenarios, which previously featured text-based operations and limited learning environments, are now becoming more open. Voice control, for example, opens up completely new ways of interacting with learning environments. In the future, exchanges with teachers and other learners will become more fluent and natural for students. People with physical disabilities, who may find text-based operations difficult, will benefit from this format.

Big Data approaches that combine learning analytics and artificial intelligence (AI) can use chatbots and e-tutors to accompany students along the learning path. In such ways, the learning environment will adapt to the needs of individual students. As this can be done using models developed in the field of AI to predict learning performance, new learning environments will offer students improved adaptive learning.

New technologies can also open and plasticize spaces via **virtual reality** and **augmented reality**. In three-dimensional space, products, machines, and processes can be experienced and manipulated, even if they do not yet exist. Thus, research-based learning can be implemented in practical ways and making use of all senses during a course of study (cf. DeYoung & Eberhart, 2018).

Of course, the idea of such learning arrangements is nothing new. To a large extent, the technology already exists (Altieri, 2018; Zick & Heinrich, 2018). However, such practices seem to be at the stage of practical testing and prototype implementation (proof-of-concept).

To make effective use of various forms of online teaching, augmented and virtual reality, and artificial intelligence, it will be necessary for **technical infrastructure and organizational processes to interact**. Teaching staff will also need training and support. Currently, the study respondents feel that bottlenecks have obstructed the provision of necessary resources and the will to plan, develop, and establish new university administrative, spatial, and learning scenarios.

For example, traditional university lecture halls will recede into the background, to be replaced with spatial planning concepts that meet the needs of modern students and teachers. Multifunctional rooms with flexible uses will enable new learning scenarios. It is possible to imagine students meeting in rooms outside the university grounds, such as "learning cafes" and "fablabs" (cf. Taddei, 2018).

Digital platforms, algorithms, and content can be developed together, taking advantage of national and international networking. Open licenses for products and services can promote the exchange and sharing of services, supporting the implementation of new learning scenarios (Ebner & Schön, 2018).

Nevertheless, the first institutional initiatives will be more expensive than previous programs, at least during the first conversion and implementation phase. The cost of the technical infrastructure will naturally increase, as will technology costs per student, which are incurred by institutions. It is important to prioritize digitization strategies at an early stage and to establish an innovation-friendly environment at each university, enabling educators to experiment with implementing new teaching scenarios, and support the development of new learning paths for students.

Some of the experts warned against assuming that all students owned the necessary hardware for learning (e.g., a laptop or mobile phone). Appropriate support programs should be established to ensure that less financially well-equipped learners are given equal opportunities to become part of the educational landscape. Barriers can arise from the availability or nonavailability of Internet access (keyword "broadband expansion"), essential hardware (e.g., technical equipment for students), and suitable platforms (e.g., "guidelines for barrier-free web content," WCAG). The experts thus addressed the important issue of the "digital divide" (Hess et al., 2016) and the danger that digitization could lead to a new set of social disadvantages if such questions are neglected.

Finally, with a view to the future, the experts stressed that, although online teaching and virtual space will be more central and important in the university of the future, **attendance phases will remain important**. The experts assumed that some universities would continue to concentrate primarily on campus-based learning in 2030. Online universities would also establish themselves. This could lead to cooperation between the two types of universities, enabling them to achieve their goals as economically as possible. Such developments could present challenges for the recognition of learning achievements, especially if parts of the learning process took place outside the higher education sector.

2.1.4.2   The Operational and Strategic Benefits of Technology in Higher Education

During the expert discussions, it quickly became clear that true innovation rarely lies in technology alone, but reflects the way in which technology is used to consistently redesign educational experiences. The programming school 42, for example, uses a classic intranet to provide educational content, which is **not, in itself, particularly innovative**. What is new about 42 is the fact that its entrance examination is accessible to candidates with no prior qualifications; during "study" periods, any examination can be repeated until a student has achieved his or her learning objective. Although this approach can only be implemented with technology, technology alone is not enough. Another essential element is openness, which makes it possible to try something new and to question the old.

In the present analysis of higher education in 2030, the influence of digital technology has to be considered on two levels. On the one hand, traditional higher education institutions will increasingly integrate digital technology into their existing processes (the "operational" approach).[6] On the other hand, technology will enable entirely new

---

[6] A mirror image of this approach can be seen in most responses to the survey of German university digitization strategies (Gilch et al., 2019), in which digitization is used mainly to improve the administration of existing processes and to increase efficiency.

models, most of which will emerge outside or on the fringes of traditional universities; these will represent a digital transformation of higher education (the "strategic" approach) (Evans & Wurster, 1997; cf. Sollosy, Guidice, & Parboteeah, 2015).

Within the framework of operational use of digital technology in existing universities, technology-adoption theory provides a useful orientation framework. It states: "The most important thing in observing [the adoption of technology] is that, at all times, the choice is not between adoption and non-adoption, but between immediate adoption and postponing the decision until later" (Hall & Khan, 2003). Perhaps no profound changes have been needed so far because environmental pressures on higher education are not yet strong enough and requirements are not yet heterogeneous enough. A key question for the future of higher education is how long this situation will persist. Like other institutions with a long tradition, the higher education system is innovation-resistant. This is not necessarily negative. It makes no sense to follow every new technology trend. On the other hand, resisting innovation may ensure that important and positive changes are driven by others, putting pressure on existing higher education structures. Although universities can use innovations from the edge to drive their own transformations, this will require an **ambitious strategic reorientation**.

The potential of the strategic approach becomes clear when considering initiatives and institutions outside existing institutions. Some education providers have emerged outside the traditional higher education sector (e.g., 42); some have developed as start-ups (e.g., Minerva) and are not subject to the usual planning processes (e.g., MIT MicroMasters); they may exist in new, separate units within a university. This is where new models will emerge that force stakeholders to question and creatively rethink many things. Radical changes are likely to affect almost all aspects of universities, from campus design to ways of undertaking, testing, and accrediting learning, and the relationship between business and education. Relevant cases are presented in the following sections of this study as explorative examples. Common to all cases is the fact that their educational provision embeds the potential of digitization.

> **Conclusion: Opportunities for Digitally Supported Higher Education 2030**
> Technological development means that future learning scenarios are possible, but will require institutional and organizational innovation, not merely the use of new technologies. The following considerations must be taken into account:
> - The impact of digital technology can be considered on two levels. On the one hand, traditional universities will increasingly integrate digital technology into existing educational processes. On the other hand, digital technology will be used to develop fundamentally new educational providers and programs. By the year 2030, these may supplement and partly replace the offerings of traditional universities.

- Technical development means that the contrast between analogue and digital learning scenarios can be dissolved. This offers opportunities to provide individualized support for student-learning paths. Learning can be independent of time and place; individual study (the study of specialist or less popular subjects) could become the norm for many students.
- With technology-based solutions, care must be taken to ensure that all students have access to technology and the technical support they need to use it. Otherwise, the digital divide may promote a new social divide.
- Through the use of digital technology, higher education providers can increasingly benefit from cooperation and exchange, jointly developing successful concepts and suitable learning materials.
- The effective use of these technologies within traditional higher education institutions will depend strongly on the capacity of institutions to implement innovation processes. Universities must be willing to make necessary resources available and to question existing administrative, spatial, and learning scenarios—or to replace them with new approaches.
- Furthermore, support will be provided for new, innovative education providers and models that can supplement the role of traditional universities.
- As a rule, innovations need spaces outside the organizational and planning processes of universities. They develop where they are protected from the "immune system" of traditional organizations. They can also be separate units within higher education institutions.

2.2   Development of Scenarios and Validation Discussions

Higher education in 2030 will be determined by the parameters listed in Sect. 2.1. Labor market requirements for new knowledge and competence will have an external impact on higher education. The reaction in higher education will be shaped by didactic models and digitally supported learning scenarios.

This complex structure of effects means that higher education will not have a single form, becoming, instead, more differentiated (Davey et al., 2018). To develop future scenarios in higher education, a literature search has provided the three approaches briefly described below:

2.2.1 Modeling that Focuses on Institutions and Governance Issues in Particular

After examining global developments in higher education, the OECD developed a four-field matrix based on two opposing pairs: the extent of globalization (global versus local) and the influence of the state (administration versus market). This resulted in the following four scenarios (OECD, 2008):

- **Higher education Inc.**—higher education with an international catchment area and market-oriented offerings. According to van der Wende, this model was the most likely future model at the time (van der Wende, 2017).
- **Open networking**—a form of higher education that focuses on stronger international cooperation (networking) and supply-oriented care. This approach has been strongly influenced by the Bologna Process, taking place in the European Higher Education Area and extending to 48 countries (European Commission/EACEA/Eurydice, 2018). A greater harmonization between systems and more use of digitization is expected to promote this process further.
- **New public responsibility**—a form of higher education that focuses on the national market and on market-oriented provisions, which must be accountable to the state. This approach reflects the increasing focus on the new management model; it includes, among other things, a performance-related allocation of funds (Orr & Jaeger, 2009).
- **Serving local communities**—a form of higher education that focuses on the national market and supply-oriented provision at the local level. This has been seen as a likely scenario in the event of a possible counter-attack against globalization (van der Wende, 2017).

2.2.2 Modeling that Focuses on Technology

The Holon IQ analysis has focused on the (expected) impact of technology on higher education (Holon IQ, 2018). It has proposed five models: Education-as-usual, Global giants, Regional rising, Peer-to-peer, and Robo Revolution. The first three models anticipate domestic changes in the higher education sector and roughly reflect the OECD models mentioned above. These contrast with the last two models, which can exist without conventional higher education. It is worthwhile to briefly present these two models:

- **Peer-to-peer**—This scenario is the other side of the OECD scenario, "open networking," since it does not involve institutions, but people, who build their own learning and cooperation networks. It proposes a module-based learning path that allows learners to collect "micro credits" as they pursue their own interests and build careers.

- **Robo Revolution**—The OECD did not consider this scenario because it paid little attention to the impact of digitization on higher education. In fact, the "Robo Revolution" is a sophisticated version of the peer-to-peer model, in which artificial intelligence and machine learning allow for better identification and presorting of learning materials, making it easier to identify relevant learning resources. Scalable personalized support can be provided by social bots.

2.2.3 Modeling that Focuses on Social Developments

The "Beyond Current Horizons" study in the UK has carried out an environmental analysis to develop three complete scenarios of future societies, from which six educational models have been extracted (Facer, 2009). For each societal scenario, two alternative models have been proposed for the education system—one with positive and the other with negative characteristics. The three scenarios bear the names: "Trust yourself," "Only connect," and "Loyalty points." It is worth presenting these scenarios and their corresponding models in more detail.

- **Trust yourself**—In this society, citizens take responsibility for themselves. There are two educational models: **informed choice** and the **independent consumer**. In the case of an "informed choice," the educational model is based on the personal learning journey of an individual supported by mentors. The focus is on the individual's journey, within a process of lifelong learning. Educational outcomes are assessed in the context of the learner's previous and subsequent learning experiences. In the case of the "independent consumer," the focus is on the independent selection of standardized learning materials. This leads to two tensions. The first tension is a tendency for learners to accept materials provided by well-known "brand names." In addition, some learners lack the support to navigate this relatively complex system, especially if their social networks are unfamiliar with it.
- **Only connect**—This society is focused on the shared task of overcoming great environmental challenges, which can only be solved collectively. It has two educational models: **integrated experience** and **service and citizenship**. In the case of "integrated experience," the educational model is more inclusive than before, with learning taking place everywhere—at work, in care, during leisure time, and in educational institutions. This model sees education as integrated; learning is a collaborative and contextual open process that extends throughout life. In the case of "service and citizenship," the dominant view is that individuals must be taught to be good citizens. Learning is increasingly seen as something that happens outside people's social context, providing necessary input for employment, work, and well-being.
- **Loyalty points**: In this society, the relationship between individuals and businesses of all kinds is increasingly codified and formalized over time. Individuals are subject to a network of memberships and associations. These cover all areas of

life, controlling, and limiting the behavior of groups and individuals: work, personal interests, healthcare, family, leisure, and consumption. In this context, the state focuses on promoting social sustainability, ensuring that the many different perspectives and priorities within society do not pull strongly in different directions. This society has two educational models: **discovery** and **diagnosis**. In the case of "discovery," the model for education involves learners moving between different groups and associations, interacting with and contributing to the various knowledge communities they encounter. Through this process, learners build a portfolio of skills and contributions that are digitally captured, authenticated, and shared. In the case of "diagnosis," the educational model analyzes each individual's skills at an early stage and predicts which links and associations will fit that person best. As a result, people make fewer efforts to develop larger networks or affiliations; instead, they aim to be successful within a limited circle of associations. This leads to a less dynamic society with a high dependence on proximal networks.

The approach that was chosen for this study also begins with learners and their learning pathways. As the analysis above has shown, **learning will be the central feature of the digital world** and the key to social participation for a wide range of people.

This approach also ties in with an idea promoted by Barnett University, which calls its concept of open higher education the "ecological university" (Barnett, 2011). Barnett distinguishes between three visions of the university: the research university—which exists "in itself," i.e., for science; the entrepreneurial university—which exists "for itself," i.e., to support a company; and the **ecological university**—which exists "for others," being open to all and open to the world.

Figure 2.5 places students at the center of the system, surrounded by appropriate higher education resources that meet their learning needs. This perspective avoids the "digital-first" approach, which was prominent in the age of e-learning—namely, the idea that education should begin with technology, rather than with users and benefits (Andersson, Alaja, & Buhr, 2016; Buhr, 2015; Howaldt & Jacobsen, 2010; Rüede & Lurtz, 2012). By contrast, this approach emphasizes the idea that social contexts, such as education, are always about social innovation—how social processes can be reconfigured to achieve goals more effectively.

According to this approach, in 2030 the higher education landscape will be formed around various learning paths taken by students. As Fig. 2.5 shows, the AHEAD concept is based on four ideal learning paths in the university landscape of 2030. The resulting models of higher education are not exclusive but will coexist because they address different needs.

The AHEAD models have been further developed and validated in various cycles by different groups of experts[7]:

- Initial development by the AHEAD team in August 2018;
- Presentation of the models and discussion, in the context of the German Higher Education Forum on Digitization topic week, in September 2018;

---

[7] See the Methods section in the Appendix.

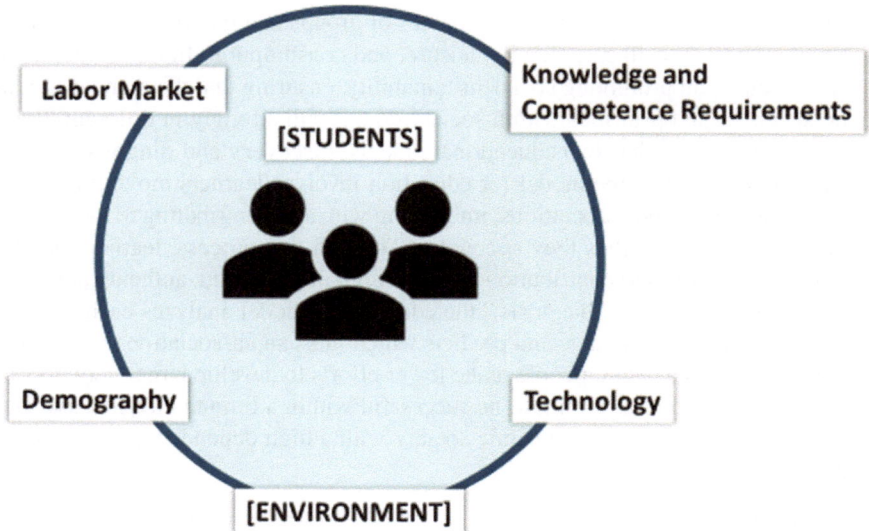

Fig. 2.5 Requirements for higher education from the perspective of students. *Source* Own illustration

- Further development and assessment from an international perspective, provided by the AHEAD Advisory Board, October 2018;
- An online survey of international experts from the higher education sector. The results of the survey are listed as exemplars in "marginal notes" in the model descriptions below.

These models are described and then characterized on the basis of their social drivers, didactic and technological solutions, and innovation potential in the next chapter.

Chapter 3
Four Models of Higher Education in 2030

Abstract This chapter provides four models of higher education for the year 2030, namely the Tamagotchi, Jenga, Lego Set, and Transformer models. The Tamagotchi model represents the classic approach to higher education, starting right after secondary school and leading up to a bachelor's or master's degree and then transitioning into employment, finishing the path of higher education. The Jenga model, while similar to Tamagotchi, appeals to nontraditional students because of its shorter learning span and focuses on later phases of self-learning and -organization. The Lego Set model is fittingly named after the individually combined modules of different sizes, making for a self-reliant and non-standardized learning path rather than one compact unit. The Transformer model represents learners whose initial phase of education may have long passed, but who return to higher education to acquire new basic knowledge or upskill their formal education. It relies on the idea that everyone must have opportunities to leave their current professional paths and change course.

Figure 3.1 shows the four learning paths in individual career. The blocks represent the main learning phases of higher education. Of course, learners may be working while they learn or pursuing other societal commitments.[1] Phases without blocks are outside the higher education system and characterized by work or other social commitments. Each learning path is named after a toy that roughly represents the main characteristics of this learning path. However, these names should not be taken too seriously; they are simply intended to help readers remember the core properties of the four models.

---

[1] Currently, approximately half of all students work at least a few hours a week during their studies (Masevičiūtė, Šaukeckienė, & Ozolinčiūtė, 2018).

© FiBS - Forschungsinstitut für Bildungs- und Sozialökonomie, and HIS-Institut für Hochschulentwicklung e.V. (HIS-HE) 2020
D. Orr et al., *Higher Education Landscape 2030*,
SpringerBriefs in Education, https://doi.org/10.1007/978-3-030-44897-4_3

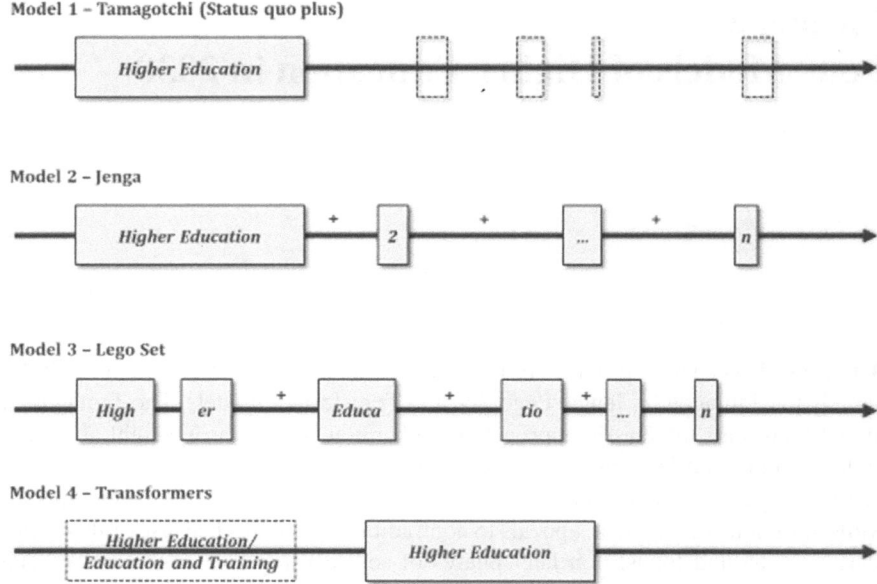

Model 1 – Tamagotchi (Status quo plus)

Model 2 – Jenga

Model 3 – Lego Set

Model 4 – Transformers

Fig. 3.1 Four learning paths in the 2030 higher education landscape. *Source* Own illustration

3.1   Brief Descriptions of the Learning Pathways[2]

3.1.1   Tamagotchi: Higher Education for a Good Start in Life

> **Tamagotchi**
>
> *A closed ecosystem that is built around individual students. The focus is on the beginning of the learning path.*

In this model, **students** are beginning their careers. Secondary school education is completed with the acquisition of higher education entrance qualifications. The transfer to the university takes place immediately afterward. Students study full time, until their three- or five-year courses end, depending on whether they are aiming for a bachelor's or master's degree. After graduation, the graduates begin their careers. The purpose of higher education is to enable graduates to obtain work-related skills and to create a knowledge base that enables them to make the transition to employment. When students graduate, learning within the higher education system is essentially finished. Most further learning is nonformal, informal, or demand-oriented, guided by

---

[2]Footnotes in the following section reproduce some comments from the international survey (see Sect. 6.1.3) on the respective models.

each individual's professional situation. Further education is undertaken but without an explicit connection to previous study phases.

This model assumes that graduates will continue to be offered a future-proof education; they will not be trained simply to meet the requirements of the current labor market but will acquire skills that enable them to help shape their environment.[3]

The **didactic concept** of the Tamagotchi model supports learning and personal development through a learning path that has clearly defined steps and results. This path continues the school-system approach previously followed. Ideally, secondary and tertiary education are well-coordinated, allowing the transfer to higher education to occur without major discontinuities. The concept supports academic orientation on the one hand and a certain degree of self-organization and independent learning on the other.

The university remains the central teaching and learning space. Students are part of a community that promotes the social inclusion of individual students. In addition to exchanging information on campus, students also learn with the support of global communication networks, simulations, and augmented reality techniques, which expand the physical learning environment. Future learning experiences in the professional world will be integrated through innovative learning spaces, such as makerspace and fablabs, but also through traditional internships.

In this model, each university is responsible for **control and coordination**, as well as the design of the degree program. The introductory phase of studies and thus the change from school to university are important points in the design.

The Tamagotchi model follows the traditional concept of higher education. It assumes that the knowledge and skills acquired at university give learners a future-proof competence profile and enable them to adapt flexibly to future requirements.

One **central factor that influences the success and attractiveness of this model** is the diversification of the student group. So far, learning has taken place in cohorts (relatively age-homogeneous groups) which generally need a certain educational background to be successful.

If universities recruit more alternative target groups, such as older students, this may lead to a fundamental change that will not reflect the Tamagotchi model approach. However, universities will have to react to the growing permeability of the higher education system by meeting the needs of diversified, often (partly) employed students more fully and precisely. As universities respond by offering more flexible courses and student-centered teaching, this model will come under pressure.

To help degree programs become more flexible, governmental steering regimes will have to adapt by reconsidering key figures relevant to the distribution of funds, such as graduates within the standard period of study. They will also have to develop clearly defined control approaches.

---

[3]Moreover, this model remains relevant to the process of preparing young scientists for academic careers.

The example of Minerva (see Case: Minerva) shows how the Tamagotchi model can be developed through innovation; here the model offers networked, campus-independent higher education in bachelor's programs, consistently exploiting technological possibilities and removing spatial restrictions. At the same time, this case succeeds in maintaining the care and support promised by the Tamagotchi model.

Case: Minerva—The World as a Campus

Relevant for the model: **Tamagotchi**

At first glance, Minerva looks like an ordinary university, and that's what it's meant to be. But if you look under the surface, you discover a whole new approach to university-organized education. Instead of a traditional campus, Minerva has a network of seven satellite locations around the world. All courses are offered online, to small groups of 20 students. Students live in shared dormitories, even though classes are held online. Minerva reveals the possibilities that exist when digitization is understood and realized in a transformative way. In this context, traditional ways of organizing education can be presented in completely new forms.

The private university was founded by Ben Nelson in 2012, with the aim of offering "Ivy League" quality education, in combination with a different concept of the learning community. Despite the central role of video-based teaching, Nelson does not believe that Minerva is innovative because of its technology. For him, the innovation began with a new pedagogy, built around 100 important ideas, which can be taught, applied, and evaluated (the list includes both patterns of critical thinking and scientific concepts). The technology is not decisive, although this approach could not be put into practice without it.

At Minerva, innovation does not end with a new video system but involves a continual questioning of what role the campus can and should play in this model. Initially, Nelson and his colleagues did not want to replace the social experience of living and learning together, but to improve it. To do this, they did not need their own canteen, lecture halls, library, or fitness facilities, as these are available in every major city and can be shared. Students develop a bond with their cohort, but not with a particular location. The university gives them opportunities to get to know about different cultures and environments.

What does teaching at Minerva look like? All courses are conducted live via video by professors working with small groups of up to 20 students. In this seminar-like approach, instruction, discussion, group work, and assessment are freely mixed—professors have access to "real-time" information on the students' learning progress and can thus adjust the pace and content. Although Nelson mainly talks about the higher quality teaching that can be achieved, another advantage is the flexibility of physical learning spaces. It is no longer necessary to invest in large lecture halls—students can log in from a café or from home—and intelligent technologies can take the strain off tutors.

Minerva is an example of how digital technology can extend a model like Tamagotchi, which is based on familiar technology. The distributed-learning approach could also be applied to the Lego and Jenga models.

3.1.2   Jenga: Higher Education as a Solid Foundation for Further Development

Jenga
Universities offer a solid foundation of knowledge to build on; this foundation can be constantly expanded by teachers.

As in the Tamagotchi model, students are expected to begin their studies immediately after obtaining university entrance qualifications. As a rule, students study full time for up to three years,[4] acquiring basic knowledge and skills. The initial university period is shorter than that in the Tamagotchi model, appealing to **nontraditional students,** for whom four or five years of study would be too long. However, this assumes that learners will expand their knowledge through additional modules over the course of their lives and after interruptions. Depending on each individual's professional situation, these modules can provide upskilling opportunities or sideways skills acquisition.

The central idea is that university studies, in the traditional model, are not flexible or integrative enough to be future-proof in a highly dynamic environment. Courses of studies must, therefore, be conceived more broadly, with a longer perspective. In the initial study phase, individuals learn the basics; these skills are then supplemented later in life. In this model, a didactic decision must initially be made to define the educational foundation needed to begin a specific career and the content that should be provided later, in shorter phases of continued education. Whether the basic foundation includes general or transversal competences or specific basic knowledge depends on the discipline and university.

It is important, however, that the **didactic concept** initially focuses on a basic phase (basic study), which supports later self-learning and self-organization. In this phase, students' learning and personal development proceed along a clear learning path, with fixed steps and clear results. In the first block phase of this model, learning takes place mainly on campus, with the support of global communication networks, simulations, and augmented reality techniques that extend the learning environment through online experiences. Through internships, makerspaces, and fablabs, early

---

[4]Like junior colleges in South Korea and so-called "accelerated degrees" in the UK.

connections to the future world of work are established. After successfully completing their studies, students leave university and enter professional life. **Universities** help to prepare for this transition and focus on this task within the Jenga model. The second learning phase consists of **several learning units**, which the learners themselves choose, often taking into account the changing competence requirements of the labor market. The short study blocks can be offered by various training providers; they can take place either on-campus or online and can also be combined.

Formal recognition of the first learning block is guaranteed. The recognition of other learning units depends on how such studies are organized within the higher education landscape. Learners will have opportunities to reach outcome-based agreements with individual higher education institutions, covering both the initial learning block and additional units. In this way, Learning Phase 1 and Learning Phase 2 can be integrated into a single study program. However, the two phases can also be accessed independently.

The Jenga model consistently responds to the needs of students and the labor market. This study design can prepare for and respond to new **needs from the world of work** without abandoning the basic structure of a university course of study.

One example, "MIT MicroMasters," represents an innovative variant of the Jenga model. After students acquire a bachelor's degree in Phase 1, their MicroMasters learning can be organized very flexibly during the second phase. MIT thus offers an innovative variant within the existing system.

One major innovation could involve developing an entire study program that would be provided by different providers during different study phases. Students would be accompanied throughout the study program, even if only the first part took place at their own universities. Under this system, universities would require digital student-administration systems and "stackable" **individual digital certificates**, which could later be used to recognize a complete course of study. The question remains whether preparatory colleges and other providers would collaborate with traditional universities to create partnerships of this type, or whether they would rather develop their own overall study/training programs.

Case: 42—Focus on Project-based Learning and Peer Evaluation

Relevant for the models: ***Tamagotchi***, ***Jenga***

Olivier Creuzet (Head of Pedagogy at 42): "We actually lie to our students. We say they will develop technical skills, but we want to develop adaption, self-learning, creativity, and other soft skills."

One characteristic of the Jenga model is direct access to the labor market. This was also the goal of "42," an innovative school for software developers in Paris (with an offshoot in the U.S.), founded in 2013 by Xavier Niel, a French multimillionaire. Access to 42 is free and organized like a computer game. Interested learners must first pass the "Piscine" (swimming pool), a kind of four-week entrance exam, which mainly tests their ability to co-work with others and apply new knowledge. Success in the Piscine is independent of existing programming skills. Each student then works on a consecutive series of projects and simultaneously provides feedback on other students' projects. As in a computer game, each project can be improved as often as necessary before students advance to the next level. This all sounds very modern, but Olivier Creuzet attributes it to a classic constructivist approach developed by Piaget and Montessori. What's new about 42 is that this approach can now be implemented cost-effectively in larger groups with the help of technology.

Most learners do not yet have a university degree; through 42, they find a direct path from secondary education to their first jobs. There are exceptions, however. Some students enter 42 to learn practical programming skills, after completing a traditional degree. Others are already working as professionals, but want to reorient themselves; a course of study at 42 may help them enter university later, as we have outlined in the Transformer model (see below). In the didactics of 42, learning processes are modeled on the work activities of programmers. For example, students use the tools and platforms they are likely to encounter in their first jobs. This approach blurs the strict separation between work and study. 42 is a direct reaction to the growing demand for software developers, which traditional universities cannot meet. As technologies are evolving rapidly, specific programming languages quickly become obsolete. The careful and therefore slow process of university-curriculum development cannot keep pace with such applications. However, for many jobs, companies do not expect a degree in computer science, but simply solid, basic knowledge (the "craft" of programming) and the ability to collaborate with others and continue learning.

42 enables students to acquire these key competences. In addition to programming, students develop skills such as self-learning and self-organization. Although these are not directly related to software, they will benefit the students in their professional lives and further studies. Although 42 aims to provide an innovative programming education, it also attaches great importance to skills such as adaptability, self-learning, creativity, and various other nontechnical social skills. These are exactly the skills that learners in the Jenga model need to create their own learning paths.

Case: MIT MicroMasters—Flexibility after the First Study Phase

*Relevant for the models: **Jenga, Lego, Transformer***

Since 2016, students who have successfully completed a series of online courses and then passed an exam under supervision have been able to spend slightly more than USD 1000 to acquire MicroMasters from the Massachusetts Institute of Technology (MIT). The first MicroMasters was developed for the supply-chain-management sector, where there was a growing need for experts that traditional universities could not meet. For example, MIT offers only 30 students the option to take a master's degree per year on campus; this number cannot easily be increased (or decreased) from one year to the next. So MIT professors decided to offer their courses online, building a new type of degree.

Although the MicroMasters is not an "official" university degree, it is recognized as a learning achievement by some large companies and 22 universities in 16 countries. Overall, 40% of MicroMasters students have more than 5 years of work experience. MicroMasters students are in their early thirties, on average; approximately half of them already have a university degree. However, more than 20% come directly to the MicroMasters program without a previous degree. Completing the full MicroMasters program takes time, initiative, and motivation. For this reason, few students successfully complete all of the courses. To date, about 1300 students have received MicroMasters from MIT. However, this total is 20 times more than the number of students on the MIT campus who are working on supply-chain master's degrees. In addition, more than 30,000 students have completed at least one online module.

The aim of the MicroMasters program was to give more people access to knowledge and to create a new form of access to the traditional MIT Master's program. However, the results have been much more interesting. Today, not only does MIT accept MicroMasters when considering applications from potential students, other universities and even employers do the same. The MicroMasters program has simply put into practice something that was difficult to organize in theory—the mutual recognition of course achievements. For example, an MIT MicroMasters can be used to apply for 69 different master's programs at 22 universities around the world, while the online courses are credited. In just a few years, a global network has emerged that combines MOOCs with traditional university degrees in this way. Since two of the universities are located in Europe, this program automatically gives students access to the European Credit Transfer and Accumulation System (ECTS), as well as eligibility in many of the 48 countries of the European Higher Education Area (EHEA). Further study is not necessarily the goal of every student, and companies have also noticed the MicroMasters. For example, General Electric, one of the largest employers in the U.S., guarantees all applicants an interview if they have a MicroMasters. This is true whether they have a (regular) university degree or not.

In the Jenga model, a MicroMasters could be one of the study blocks needed to acquire and carry out a job. However, the case is also relevant to the Lego model, as a single study block among others, and to the Transformer model as an alternative path into higher education.

3.1.3 Lego: Higher Education as a Kit

> **Lego**
> *The course of study is not completed as a compact unit but consists of individually combined modules of different sizes.*

In this model, **students** are highly motivated and self-reliant and prefer an individual, non-standardized learning path that meets their learning needs and interests fully.[5] They combine various learning units, which are offered online and on-campus by different universities and new educational providers. The chain of learning units forms each student's personal study process. This model is also characterized by frequent changes between phases of employment and learning.

The central idea of Lego is to cater to a group of learners who are strongly self-motivated and able to create individual study programs that meet their own needs. This approach can succeed, at least for the time being, in professions in which specific skills, such as software development, are in more demand than professional qualifications. The primary aim is to acquire knowledge and skills that can be used directly for personal purposes. Learners may have different motivations for adopting this approach.

Lego students build their own individual study programs out of various learning units. They are supported by employers, representatives of occupational groups (who define occupational standards), and (where available) universities (and other service providers), which design learning paths, even for learners who may not be enrolled. In the best case, the **didactic design** of learning units takes into account the students' practical experience, appreciating that times spent not learning may have a significant impact on students' learning behavior.

The **recognition** of learning units depends on the general structure of recognition within the higher education landscape. For example, students can enter into a learning agreement with a single institution, based on learning outcomes that combine various learning units. However, it is also possible to combine learning achievements into an academic degree and to have them recognized, if necessary with certain conditions. In this way, people who cannot or do not want to make a long-term commitment in advance, for family or professional reasons, as in the Tamagotchi model, can nevertheless complete their university studies.

---

[5] At present, several models follow a similar approach. In Austria, for example, students can engage in "irregular studies" ("*Studium irregulare*"). However, these studies must correspond to a diploma, bachelor's or master's degree and "be equivalent to a relevant course of study;" see: https://www.uni.at/studium/individuelle-studien/. In Great Britain it is possible to obtain a so-called "open degree" from the Open University UK (Cooke, Lane, & Taylor, 2018).

Case: DNB—Learning Culture as the Central Strategy of a Company

*Relevant for the models: **Lego, Transformer***

Universities do not play a major role in the ambitious (further) education strategy of DNB, Norway's leading financial enterprise. In the past, DNB sent a few hundred employees per year to bachelor's degree programs at traditional universities. Today, DNB has more than 9000 employees, who have constant free access to a vast amount of digital-educational content. Most employees decide for themselves what content they want to learn and how much time they want to invest in training. Instead of investing a relatively large amount of money in training a small number of employees, DNB uses digital technologies to reach out to all employees with a wide range of educational opportunities. DNB shows how the Lego model can be supported within a large business enterprise. At the same time, DNB also provides employees with many years of work experience and an introduction to a new type of higher education (the Transformer model—see below).

Almost all aspects of traditional financial business are changing rapidly, due to the use of digital technology. In future, sales staff will collaborate with chatbots to advise customers. The customers will be better informed and able to approach the company with clear ideas and wishes. To achieve this, employees must learn to use digital technologies for consulting and communication. However, it is no longer enough to have a single learning phase in the course of a whole life. Many fields of activity change continuously—faster than universities can develop suitable educational offers. Furthermore, DNB is not at all interested in its employees being able to obtain new university degrees; it wants them to be able to apply new competences and skills.

For DNB, learning is a strategic priority and part of its corporate culture. Educational innovation begins with technology—a user-friendly mobile learning platform, on which all DNB-selected learning opportunities are accessible—strategically anchored within the organization. DNB's Senior Vice President for Learning & Development meets with the management every six weeks to present results and approve new projects. In addition, the firm encourages workers to suggest new learning opportunities. Some meeting rooms can be quickly converted into "lounges," where employees can meet to learn together. If such innovative openness is lived across all levels of an organization, a new learning culture can develop. It is worth the effort since companies that are constantly learning are better able to benefit from the digital transformation of their industries.

The example of DNB shows that the increasingly narrow demarcation between work and higher education is likely to become a major driving force for change in the higher education system. DNB's strategic focus on education is still somewhat unusual. If Norway's leading financial institution is successful in its ambitious education strategy, however, other large companies can be expected to follow. Traditional higher education can support these processes by providing flexible programs (while closely observing and exploring the latest developments in finance), but this requires more flexible educational provision and a new and open relationship with the economy.

The Lego model closes **gaps in the conventional range of training** offered by higher education institutions which, due to the dynamics of social change, are not covered by traditional bachelor's degree programs. The small-scale combination of different courses makes it possible for learners to respond to short-term demands and to acquire very individual qualifications. Although the DNB case (see Case: DNB) shows how this can be achieved from an entrepreneurial perspective, learning within the DNB system has not yet been recognized by the formal education system.

3.1.4 Transformer: Higher Education as an Opportunity for Change

Transformer

The students in this model do not enter universities directly as school-leavers but have already acquired their own professional identities and life experiences, which they bring to their studies.

In this model, schooling and the initial phase of education (possibly including higher education) have long since passed. **Learners** return to higher education either to acquire new basic knowledge and skills (side-skilling) or to improve their level of formal education (upskilling). They may be motivated by the need to prepare for a career change or to acquire higher qualifications. In this model, learners study relatively intensively over a period of three to five years and complete their tertiary education with the expectation of returning to or re-entering the labor market. The Transformer model enables individual learners to take advantage of opportunities to adapt their knowledge and skills profiles.

The central idea of this model is that, in the future, everyone must have opportunities to leave their chosen path in life and to change course. Options to participate in higher education and educational aspirations should not be determined by age or biography.

The **didactic concept** behind the Transformer model supports learning and personal development, through clearly defined steps and results. As learners begin higher education many years after leaving the formal education system, they need considerable support. At the same time, these learners have acquired knowledge, skills, and experience through their previous roles and can apply them to their learning. A careful balance is therefore needed between academic support, guidance, and independent learning to achieve individual goals.

Universities are responsible for the **control and coordination**, and also the design, of the study program. The didactics take into account the knowledge, competence, and experience profiles of learners before they begin the course. However, credit for or recognition of previous achievements is rarely provided. Once progress has been made in this field, far shorter study courses should be possible. During the course of their studies, students acquire increasing control over their own learning paths; after an initial phase of the study, the proportion of **self-regulated learning** increases.

Learning takes place mainly on campus, with the support of global communication networks, simulations, and augmented reality techniques, which extend the learning environment through online experiences. Further learning spaces can be integrated into the learning experience through internships, makerspaces, and fablabs. Compatibility with the demands of work-life is achieved, above all, by extending the standard (maximum) period of study and by offering online course units.

Changes in the labor market represent an **essential driver** of the Transformer model, as they make it necessary for learners to expand their competence and knowledge profiles or to look for new fields of activity. Ultimately, this model offers a basic, work-life-oriented course of study that meets the needs of an older target group; its flexible study organization and didactic approach respond effectively to learners who may not have experienced active learning practice for many years.

3.2 A Detailed Analysis of the Models of Higher Education in 2030

The following section describes the models in more detail, exploring central aspects identified in preliminary studies (see Sect. 2.1).

3.2.1 Environmental Requirements and Models

Tamagotchi corresponds to the current model of higher education. In relation to individual learner biographies, it fits between the completion of secondary education and the beginning of tertiary (higher) education. This model will still be relevant in 2030, primarily because of increasing demand for highly qualified employees. This will continue a trend that has been observed since 1990. Members of our society have an ever-higher level of education, with a graduate rate of over 40% in the OECD average for people in the 25–34 age group in 2016 (see Fig. 3.2).[6] Higher education remains a good investment for the state and for graduates who, among other things,

---

[6]Initial FiBS forecasts assume that the growth trend among first-year female students in Germany will continue until 2030.

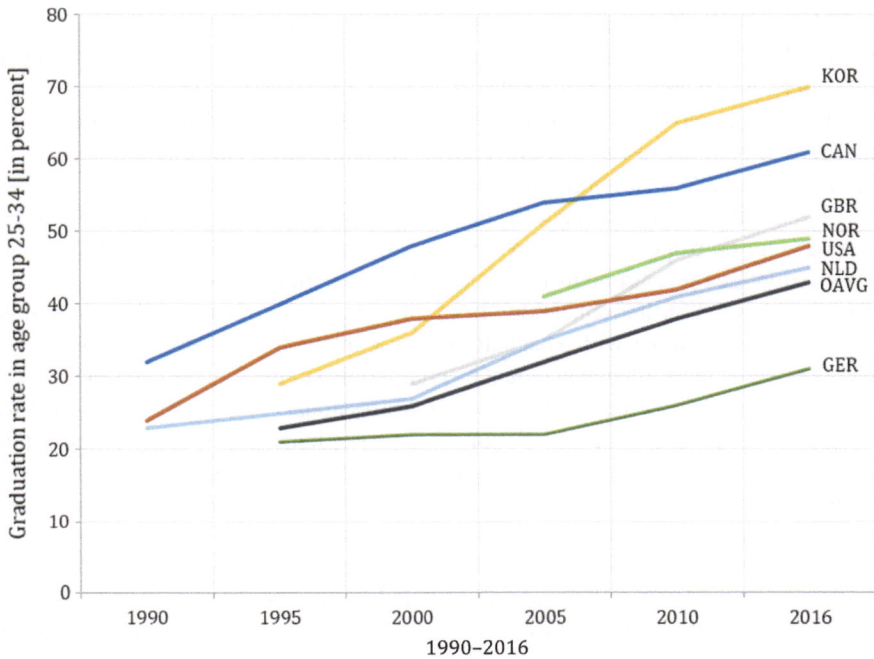

Fig. 3.2 Graduation rate in the 25–34 age group (selection of countries), 1990–2016. *Source* OECD database, population with higher education, ISCED 2011 5-8. *KOR* South Korea, *CAN* Canada, *GBR* United Kingdom, *NOR* Norway, *NLD* Netherlands, *OAVG* OECD average, *GER* Germany

earn better incomes and are less likely to become unemployed than nonacademics (European Commission/EACEA/Eurydice, 2018; OECD, 2018a). This pattern is likely to persist in a digitized world.

The Tamagotchi model focuses on providing basic knowledge and skills. If we assume that this is the only way to achieve higher (academic) qualifications, courses of study and programs must provide the knowledge and skills that learners need to transition to most high-level professions. Since this function can only be fulfilled to a limited extent if study programs change slowly, while the economy changes rapidly, debates about the "qualification deficit" and the "employability" of graduates will continue to challenge this form of higher education.

Economic developments and the interplay between economic dynamism in times of digitization and demographic shifts toward older populations suggest that access to higher education will need to be expanded. This model will not serve people who wish or need to study later in life. This is not a new challenge for higher education; it represents a line of action in the Bologna Process. However, the Tamagotchi model has not yet found an effective solution (Orr & Mishra, 2015). This model is therefore likely to cause further tensions, related to the question of whether university providers can afford to ignore societal expectations to offer extended learning opportunities. New and more innovative formats must focus on didactics, the commitment of learners, and flexible learning paths (Unger & Zaussinger, 2018).

Although **Jenga** fills the same gap between secondary and tertiary education, the Jenga model addresses a slightly different future problem. There is already a trend toward academization in the health sector and education, among other fields. This trend will become stronger in the future, as occupational profiles are created in fields that correspond to intermediate or higher level qualifications. The Jenga model addresses this problem by offering a shorter initial period of study, while also considering "further education" from the perspective of the profession. In this way, it enables a learner with a bachelor's degree in nursing to acquire an additional master's degree in health management by completing study modules and blocks. The demand for employees with higher levels of professional competence, in addition to social and emotional competence, is sure to increase. Jenga provides a solution to the qualification problem. Complete study programs can be designed to develop basic levels of professional competence; learners can then acquire or enhance context-related competences in a reflective way while working.

For industries that are already knowledge- and research-intensive, Jenga addresses the growing need to constantly update knowledge and competences during periods of professional activity. Continuing education takes place in close cooperation with the Alma Mater and continues to have an academic character, which is characteristic of this labor market field.

Lego responds to the small but important segment of the labor market that is powerfully driven by innovation and new developments. Traditional courses of study are too slow in this area; this model is demand-oriented and cross-disciplinary, allowing learners to acquire knowledge and skills efficiently. This sector is likely to become more important in the future. Through additive manufacturing (such as 3D printing), it will soon be possible to design very lean and efficient production processes, which will enable even small companies to compete effectively. Such companies, which operate smaller and faster in the market, will value opportunities for their employees to gain selective internal qualifications. In addition, the development of products and services will place increasingly specific demands on knowledge and skills that can no longer be provided by individuals but must be provided by teams of people working together. Partial knowledge and competence gaps in such teams can be filled selectively, using the Lego model. The same requirements also apply to freelancers, who frequently work in virtual teams. In fact, some co-working spaces already offer educational programs (Horn, 2018).

Transformer addresses two major developments. On the one hand, career changes are becoming more frequent; on the other hand, demographic changes mean that older citizens need new educational opportunities in order to keep pace with changes in their roles and careers. Although Transformer is intended for learners who need close didactic control and coordination during their studies, it recognizes that older learners can draw on life and work experiences.

3.2.2   *Didactic and Technological Features of the Models*

The didactic starting points for **Tamagotchi** are a set of defined learning goals, which shape the curriculum and are taught to students. The first phase of education and the transition from school to university are important in this model. Future didactic support for learning processes can be improved through digitization. In the future, the selected teaching and learning methods will be evidence-based and congruent with learning objectives, in line with constructive alignment. By closely monitoring the learning process of the students, through many guidelines, handouts, and an optimal orchestration of different methods, Tamagotchi reduces dropout rates and increases success rates. The teaching is largely uniform and geared toward average students. Learning as a specific competence has already been acquired in school.

This model builds on the learning style prevalent in schools. New educational technologies are mainly used to develop optimal teaching/learning processes. As a result, digital media are added to regular teaching events, such as lectures, seminars, and exercises. Online versions of the bridge offer support learners during the introductory phase of their studies. Learning environments become the central control instrument. Models that predict learning outcomes, developed using artificial intelligence, offer improved adaptive learning experiences. However, the challenge remains to embed such innovations in the existing and restrictive framework of university governance and institutional culture.

From a didactic point of view, **Jenga** has two phases. The first phase is similar to the Tamagotchi model, although it focuses more on the transition between education and profession. In the second phase, learners search actively for offers, after successfully completing courses of study that have met their needs, both in terms of content and time flexibility. Higher education providers can thus build on a foundation of knowledge in the second phase, while also relying on the learning style learned during the first degree.

In contrast to the first learning phase, second-phase learning content is provided through differentiated and specialized modules, which become increasingly fragmented. However, the type of learning undertaken is based on Phase 1 of this model.

Tension arises in this model when higher education institutions want to attract their own alumni into Phase 2 studies (as with the MIT MicroMasters), but must respond to their former students' individual needs by providing knowledge and competence levels and more flexible forms of provision. While Tamagotchi offers a foundation of knowledge and competence, here learners want knowledge that is relevant to their current activities. Didactic offers from nonuniversities are likely to be competitive or even to have an advantage over those of established universities.

It seems logical that Phase 2 educational offers should move into virtual space, given the changed framework conditions of former students, who now have jobs and families. In these learning phases, attendance times must be reduced or even bundled.

As a result, technical requirements will increase. Institutions must prepare teaching and learning content for the virtual space, providing systems that enable online learning phases and opportunities. Webinars, interactive videos, and virtual reality scenarios will be as commonplace as opportunities to virtually book, consume, and conclude these offers. Didactically, this model will open up new scenarios. Virtual tutoring and peer support will become far more important. This model will also require completely new organizational measures, to cope with digital certificates, digital payment systems, and a completely digital student-administration framework.

The predominant didactic principle in the **Lego** model is self-regulated learning. Learners actively seek offers that meet their needs, both in terms of content and methodology. Learning content is offered through more differentiated, specialized, and fragmented modules.

The predominant didactic principle in this model is each student's own identity and sense of "self." Students choose their own learning paths and compile individual curricula that reflect their own needs. As the research findings of distance-learning and continuing education studies have shown, time and time again, this model is a didactic prerequisite, since learners must have an established learning competence, as well as a willingness to learn.

At the same time, this model poses a challenge by relegating higher education institutions to the background. Educational providers are, above all, providers of individualized and individualizable learning spaces; they are also educational consultants. Digital tools will help students choose and organize their studies, and monitor their learning performance. This places the methods of learning analytics in the foreground. Digital platforms offer opportunities for national and international networking and exchanges with other students.

Certificates and digital proofs of competence (such as open badges) provide important documentation of learning performance (Orr & Buchem, 2019). The desire for security may foster the use of institution-independent storage locations, such as blockchain technology, for storing documents (Grech & Camilleri, 2017).

In the **Transformer** model, students have a wide range of prior knowledge that they can apply to their studies, and for which they may want recognition and appreciation. At the same time, the experience of learning in formal contexts is a distant memory; in most cases, this type of learning practice is no longer available. This model must, therefore, create a uniform ability to study, while also taking greater account of individual learning interests. It makes sense to engage participants in helping to define their own learning goals, adapted from the group. The exchange of and reflection on other experiences and backgrounds play an important role in this model. Individual lessons are tailored less to individual needs than to the interests of the group. The didactics must find a suitable balance between control and self-responsibility.

Since the content can be adapted to suit the current group of students, this model places the highest demands on the didactic competence of teachers. The Transformer model must also accommodate changes in learning by providing multifunctional learning spaces. Such spaces can be used flexibly, as traditional lecture halls, workshops, and group workrooms.

Given the average age of students, a high proportion of part-time learners can be expected. Attendance times must, therefore, be shorter than those in the Tamagotchi model. In addressing technical challenges, a combination of the Tamagotchi and Lego models is likely to be formative.

Table 3.1 provides an overview of the didactic and technological features of the models.

Table 3.1 Differences in the didactic and technological aspects of the four models

Differentiation criteria	Tamagotchi	Jenga	Lego	Transformer
Instructional design	Provided by the teacher	Provided by the teacher	Self-organized	Mixed, adapted to students but designed by teachers
Orientation of teaching content	Designed for the average student	Highly individual, but with a uniform starting point	Highly individual, with no uniform starting point	Collective, teaching content is adapted to a specific group of students
Student/teacher ratio	Students expect teachers to set and control the learning process	Students still expect significant input from teachers, but more in their professional role as experts than as classroom teachers. Students have greater personal responsibility for learning	Students control the learning process themselves and seek help from teachers when they feel it is necessary	Initially, the role of the teacher in the learning process is stronger; later the teacher is more important as an expert
Student group	Homogeneous	Heterogeneous	Extremely heterogeneous	Extremely heterogeneous
Technology	Enrichment in the classroom, educational data-mining, learning analytics for evidence-based learning	Enrichment model with 1:1 mirroring into the virtual world	Highly digitized	Hybrid form, high demands on multifunctional learning spaces
Digital learning scenarios (according to Wannemacher 2016)	Enrichment, game, and simulation	Integration, interaction, and collaboration, self-study, online learning	Personalization, self-study, online learning, open educational practice	Interaction and collaboration, open educational practice

Source Own illustration

Chapter 4
Outlook on a New University Landscape in 2030

Abstract Reflecting the change in perspective taken in this book, our survey put questions about institutional support, governance, quality assurance or financial issues aside. Moreover, digitization is not only a technical innovation but always a social one as well. This fundamental change of perspective leads to questions such as "What does the learner need?" that universities will have to face in the future. Within the survey, international experts were requested to assess the quantitative success of the different learning pathways, distributing current and future students among the four models. Unsurprisingly, the "new" learning paths were expected to become more important, although the actual prospective importance of these learning paths will depend on the supply and demand for academic studies, allowing decision-makers to rethink the educational designs based on the AHEAD modeling.

4.1 A New Focus on Learning Pathways in the Era of Digitization

To Lego: *"I think it is an interesting, innovative, and sustainable model! However, the German university landscape is neither prepared nor positioned for this in the short nor medium term."*
On the whole approach: *"We need more and more of such approaches in higher education.*
Thinking outside of the existing, firm, and relatively standardized systems."
Source: anonymous quotes from the international survey.

The four learning paths of the AHEAD study were developed during the summer of 2018; they have subsequently been discussed, in various discussion groups, by university representatives, students, political decision-makers, and business people. The vision of a higher education landscape designed around the learner spurred

© FiBS - Forschungsinstitut für Bildungs- und Sozialökonomie, and HIS-Institut
für Hochschulentwicklung e.V. (HIS-HE) 2020
D. Orr et al., *Higher Education Landscape 2030*,
SpringerBriefs in Education, https://doi.org/10.1007/978-3-030-44897-4_4

discussions in a very constructive way. Questions about institutional support, governance, and quality assurance, as well as the institutional financing required for restructuring and infrastructure, would normally shape any debate about the future of higher education or higher education institutions. In this case, these topics were moved to second place, reflecting the change in perspective.

Questions of digitization also benefit from a change of perspective. The current debate on digitization in social processes aims to shift from a technology-first approach, which originates with technology and then searches for applications, to the view that digitization is always a social innovation. Daniel Buhr emphasizes this distinction in his position paper "Social Innovation Policy for Industry 4.0" (cf. Andersson et al., 2016; Buhr, 2015):

> Social innovations have a decisive influence on whether a technical invention becomes a widespread innovation (according to Schumpeter), along which paths and channels it spreads (diffuses), and what effect it unfolds in the process. A social innovation is a targeted reconfiguration of social practices with the aim of better solving or satisfying problems or needs than is possible on the basis of established practices, and thus contributing to social progress.

The Vice-Presidents of IT systems and the so-called CIOs (Chief Information Officers) of universities now emphasize this changed perspective: "When implementing digitization, we must focus on the users and no longer on departmental silos. What does the individual need?"—says Hans Pongratz from TU Munich (Kaufmann, 2019, p. 6f.). The present study goes one step further, asking: What does the learner need?

The practical examples detailed above (Minerva, 42, MIT MicroMasters, and DNB) show how technology can be fully embedded in educational initiatives. They provide examples of a strategic approach that is not additive and does not attempt to embed technology in old structures, without significant reforms.

4.2 The Future Relevance of Learning Pathways for the Higher Education Landscape of 2030

In the various expert interviews, participants were asked what proportion of students was following these learning paths today, as well as will be in 2030. There were major differences of opinion in each group, but the experts showed particular interest in the Jenga and Lego models, which many saw as offering future promise. At the same time, many people commented that the classical model of higher education (in this case, Tamagotchi) would change considerably during the next decade.

The survey of international experts carried out between November 2018 and January 2019 also asked participants how to assess the quantitative significance of various learning pathways. Experts and stakeholders were asked to distribute current students and the future students of 2030 among the four learning paths.[1] Figure 4.1 shows the trend of responses. These initial assessments are not surprising. They

---

[1]Unfortunately, few survey participants were willing to answer this question. Obviously, many people found it difficult to allocate students to different learning paths, in accordance with this new

Assessment of the importance of the respective learning pathways in 2018 (left) and 2030 (right)

a) *Estimated share of students in 2018. The distance between the lines shows the range in which half of the assessments lie.*

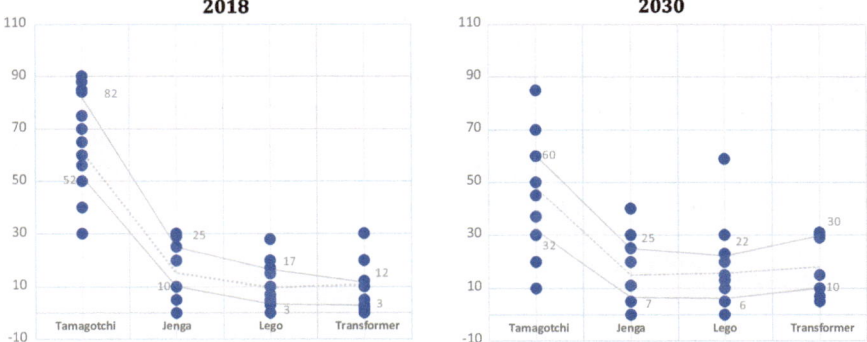

b) Mean value of the assessments for the respective learning pathways (size of the respective blocks represents the expected proportion of students).

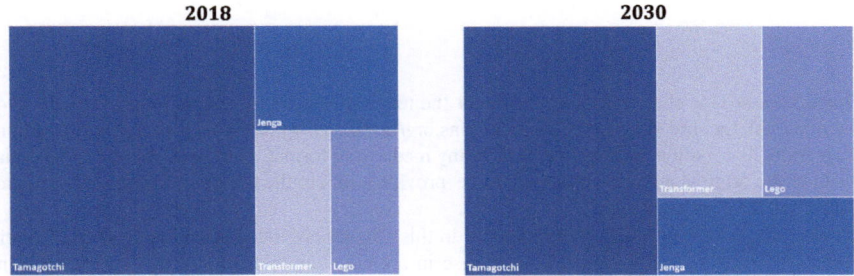

Fig. 4.1 Assessments on the current and future significance of the four learning paths. *Source* Own illustration

show that all three of the "newer" learning paths (Jenga, Lego, and Transformer) are expected to become more important, while Tamagotchi will lose some of its relevance.

However, the actual importance of each learning path will depend on both supply and demand. This means that political decision-makers, university authorities, and a range of other educational institutions should rethink the design of their educational offers and accompanying services, on the basis of AHEAD modeling. In this way, they can develop new strategies. Of course, educational institutions will be free to

perspective. More than 800 people visited the survey website and 28 people completed the survey, but only 14 were willing to answer this particular question. Their assessments are nevertheless important for explorative studies such as this one. In addition, these subjective assessments roughly reflect the opinions that project team members expressed during personal discussions.

provide a range of different learning paths.[2] For this purpose, the AHEAD learning paths offer initial goal-orientation patterns.

Over the past 20 years, the new public management model has become the focus of higher education policy measures and strategies (Jongbloed, 2015). The processes used to make courses more flexible and individualized have been partly restricted by this focus (Henderikx & Jansen, 2018, p. 78 ff; Orr & Usher, 2018). At this point, it may be helpful to consider the United Nations' educational goal 4.3 as a touchstone for higher education in Germany and Europe: "To ensure equal access for all women and men to affordable and high-quality technical, vocational, and tertiary education, including university education, by 2030" (United Nations, 2015) and to use digitization to effectively achieve this goal.

Correction to: Higher Education Landscape 2030

Dominic Orr◉, Maren Luebcke, J. Philipp Schmidt,
Markus Ebner◉, Klaus Wannemacher◉, Martin Ebner◉,
and Dieter Dohmen

Correction to:
**D. Orr et al., *Higher Education Landscape 2030*,
SpringerBriefs in Education,
https://doi.org/10.1007/978-3-030-44897-4**

The original version of the book was inadvertently published with wrong corresponding author. The role of corresponding author for all chapters should have been Dieter Dohmen, not Dominic Orr, which has now been updated and approved by the authors.

The updated version of the book can be found at
https://doi.org/10.1007/978-3-030-44897-4

Appendix

Methodological Notes

Cooperation with the Advisory Board

The Advisory Board[1] consisted of the following seven members:

- **South Korea**, Ki-Sang Song, Director of the Institute "Computers in Education," Korea National University of Education.
  Prof. Song is a member of UNESCO's expert group on educational technology and, with the support of the Korean research community, is conducting a project on learning analysis in education.
- **Norway**, Elisabeth Hovdhaugen, Senior Researcher at the Nordic Institute for Studies in Innovation, Research, and Education.
  Dr. Hovdhaugen is an international expert in higher education and participates in the Norwegian Research Council funded project "BRAIN - Barriers and Drivers in Adult Education in Acquiring Competences and Innovative Activities."
- **Netherlands**, Fred de Vries, Program Director Digital Education at Saxion University of Applied Science.
  Dr. de Vries is also involved in supporting the development of strategies for the digital university and the European project "Higher Education Online - MOOCs the European Way."
- **USA** and **Canada**, Alex Usher, President of Higher Education Strategy Associates.
  Alex Usher is an expert in the development of higher education in Canada and the USA and a founding member of the Academic Ranking and Excellence of the IREG International Observatory.

---

[1] External link: https://ahead.tugraz.at/en/our-team/.

© FiBS - Forschungsinstitut für Bildungs- und Sozialökonomie, and HIS-Institut für Hochschulentwicklung e.V. (HIS-HE) 2020
D. Orr et al., *Higher Education Landscape 2030*,
SpringerBriefs in Education, https://doi.org/10.1007/978-3-030-44897-4

- **Great Britain**, Prof. Martin Weller, Professor of Educational Technology, Teaching and Learning Innovation and Director of the Open Education Research Hub at the Open University, UK.
  Prof. Weller has recently become a Principal Fellow of the Higher Education Academy in Great Britain, which thereby honors his outstanding teaching activities.
- **World Bank**, Nina Arnhold, Senior Education Specialist, World Bank.
  The focus of Dr. Arnhold is on Europe and Central Asia with topics such as competence requirements for higher education in the context of university administration, strategy development, and digitization.
- **Germany**, Prof. Ingo Rollwagen, Professor of Management in the Creative and Science Industry at the Fresenius University of Applied Sciences.
  Dr. Rollwagen previously worked as an expert for Corporate Foresight, Technology and Education for Deutsche Bank Research and the Alfred Herrhausen Gesellschaft, Deutsche Bank's international forum.

In the course of the study, the members were advised via video-conferencing about the task of the study and the fine-tuning of the content.

Following the development of the four learning paths, a two-day workshop with the experts was held in Berlin on October 15/16, 2018. The aim of the workshop was the validation and further elaboration of the concept. The meeting was very fruitful. The advisors found the four learning paths good and supported us in further elaboration.

"Fragmented Worlds" Event

The "Fragmented Worlds" event[2] took place as part of the "Shaping the Digital Turn"[3] topic week of the "Hochschulforum Digitalisierung" on September 26, 2018, and was very well attended. We had over 150 registrations and sent 110 confirmations (40 people on the waiting list). About 70 people took part. At the event, we introduced the topic and then presented the four models in small groups.

---

[2]External link (in German): https://hochschulforumdigitalisierung.de/de/zersplitterte-welten-projektvorstellung-ahead.

[3]See: https://hochschulforumdigitalisierung.de/de/zersplitterte-welten-projektvorstellung-ahead (last viewed 08.05.2019).

The participants had the opportunity to listen to short "Lightning Talks" on the respective models of the AHEAD study and to discuss them with a team member. In these group discussions, it was also asked to indicate the proportion of students that the participants expect for the respective model in 2030. In each group, there was a dispersion, but the tendency was toward Jenga and Lego—see next page.

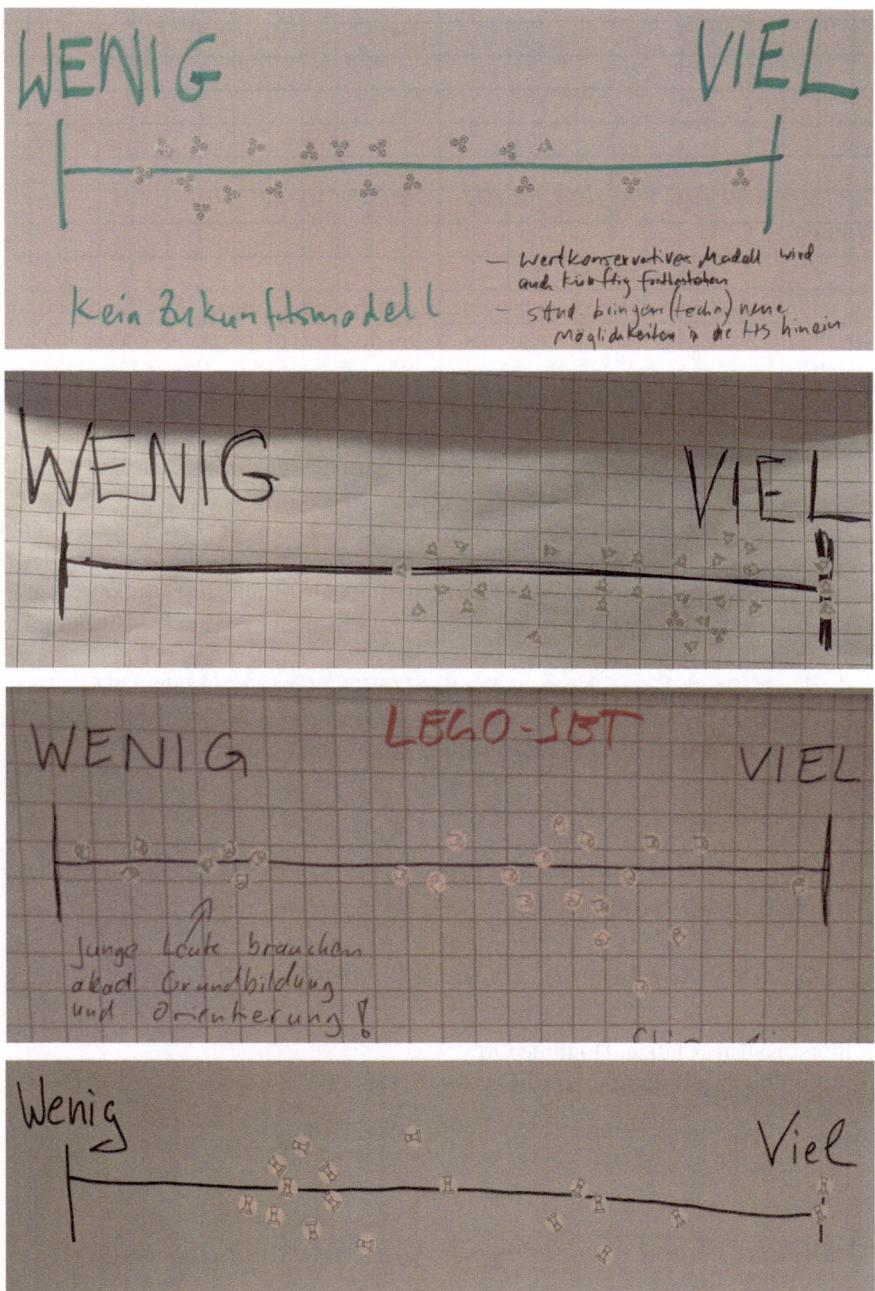

The pictures above (Source: own photographs) show a survey conducted with participants of the group discussions. The participants were asked to estimate the demand each of the four different models will generate in the future, ranging from low ("wenig") to high ("viel"). While "Tamagotchi" and "Transformer" lean more toward low demand, "Lego" and particularly "Jenga" are estimated by the participants to be the models in high demand in the future.

Background Information on the Anonymous International Survey

An anonymous international survey in English and German was launched on November 24, 2018. An international social media campaign accompanied the launch.

The survey presented the respective models in some paragraphs. Participants were asked for their assessment of their suitability for certain student groups (free text). Subsequently, the participants were asked to distribute all students currently and in the year 2030 among the four learning paths.

The perception of the survey was relatively high. About 800 people have visited the survey home page. However, the answers to the questions with 28 completed questionnaires were significantly lower (including in the English [German] version: 542 [43] visits to the introductory page, 63 [27] aborts of the survey, 18 [10] complete participants). These persons came from China, Colombia, Germany (12 persons), the Netherlands, South Korea, Norway, Scotland (UK), Slovenia, and the USA.

Students took part in the German survey and international university experts including a former Minister of Science took part in the English survey.

Detailed Descriptions of Developments in Individual Areas (Background Studies)

A1 Literature Analysis on Higher Education and its Future

Authors: Katrin Schulze, Dominic Orr
Please follow this link (in German):

* https://cloud.tugraz.at/index.php/s/A9RPHWeFHFJaoHg

A2 Knowledge and Competence Requirements Within a Digital Society

Author: Dominic Orr
Please follow this link (in German):

* https://cloud.tugraz.at/index.php/s/Tq7ZL8L3cRqbZkJ

A3 University Teaching Challenges Within a Digital Society

Authors: Klaus Wannemacher, Maren Luebcke
Please follow this link (in German):

- https://cloud.tugraz.at/index.php/s/fx8ALPYRF9DMCfR

A4.1 Technological Requirements for Higher Education

Authors: Markus Ebner, Martin Ebner
Please follow this link (in German):

- https://cloud.tugraz.at/index.php/s/TPW9476aYM5SAR2

A4.2 Digital Technology—The Outward View

Author: J. Philipp Schmidt
Please follow this link (in German):

- https://cloud.tugraz.at/index.php/s/824o9qigcyzNDJq

References

Adams Becker, S., Cummins, M., Davis, A., Freeman, A., Hall Gieseinger, C., & Ananthanarayanan, V. (2017). *NMC horizon report higher education edition 2017*. ISBN 978-0-9977215-7-7.

Altieri, P. (2018). *Let's stop calling everything AI: What automation in higher Ed looks like today*. Retrieved from https://www.signalvine.com/higher-education/education-design-lab-ai-and-higher-ed

Amanatidou, E., Butter, M., Carabias, V., Könnölä, T., Leis, M., Saritas, O., ... van Rij, V. (2012). On concepts and methods in horizon scanning: Lessons from initiating policy dialogues on emerging issues. *Science and Public Policy, 39*, 208–221. https://doi.org/10.1093/scipol/scs017

Andersson, L. F., Alaja, A., & Buhr, D. (2016). *Policies for innovation in times of digitalization*. Arena idé, Friedrich Ebert Stiftung, Kalevi Sorsa Foundation. Retrieved from http://arenaide.se/wp-content/uploads/sites/2/2016/09/policies-for-innovation-in-times-of-digitalization-160929.pdf

Barnett, R. (2011). The coming of the ecological university. *Oxford Review of Education, 37*(4), 439–455. https://doi.org/10.1080/03054985.2011.595550

Barr, R. B., & Tagg, J. (1995). From teaching to learning—A new paradigm for undergraduate education. *Change, 27*(6), 12–26.

Baumgartner, P. (2018). *3 plus 10 Thesen zu gesellschaftlichen Trends und der zukuenftigen Rolle der Hochschulen* (Diskussionspapier No. 4). Retrieved from https://hochschulforumdigitalisierung. de/sites/default/files/dateien/Diskussionspapier4_3plus_10_Thesen_zu_gesellschaftlichen_ Trends_und_der_zukuenftigen_Rolle_der_Hochschulen.pdf

Bessen, J. (2015). *Learning by doing: The real connection between innovation, wages, and wealth*. Yale University Press.

Bidarra, J., & Rusman, E. (2017). A pedagogical model for science education: Bridging formal and informal learning contexts through a blended learning approach. *Open Learning: The Journal of Open, Distance and e-Learning, 32*(1), 6–20. https://doi.org/10.1080/02680513.2016.1265442

Blossfeld, H.-P., Bos, W., Daniel, H.-D., Hannover, B., Köller, O., Lenzen, D., ... Wößmann, L. (2017). *Bildung 2030—veränderte Welt. Fragen an die Bildungspolitik* (Vereinigung der Bayrischen Wirtschaft e.V., Ed.). Waxmann Verlag.

Brennen, J. S., & Kreiss, D. (2016). Digitalization. In *The international encyclopedia of communication theory and philosophy* (pp. 1–11). Hoboken, NJ: Wiley. https://doi.org/10.1002/ 9781118766804.wbiect111

Buhr, D. (2015). *Soziale Innovationspolitik für die Industrie 4.0*. Friedlich-Ebert-Stiftung. Retrieved from http://library.fes.de/pdf-files/wiso/11302.pdf

Castells, M. (2010). *The rise of the network society*. Massachusetts: Blackwell Publishing. https:// doi.org/10.2307/1252090

© FiBS - Forschungsinstitut für Bildungs- und Sozialökonomie, and HIS-Institut
für Hochschulentwicklung e.V. (HIS-HE) 2020
D. Orr et al., *Higher Education Landscape 2030*,
SpringerBriefs in Education, https://doi.org/10.1007/978-3-030-44897-4

CEDEFOP. (2018). *Insights into skill shortages and skill mismatch.* Publications Office of the European Union. https://doi.org/10.2801/645011

Cedefop. (2009). *The shift to learning outcomes.* Cedefop.

Cerwal, P. (Ed.). (2017). *Ericsson mobility report.* Retrieved from https://www.ericsson.com/assets/local/mobility-report/documents/2017/ericsson-mobility-report-june-2017.pdf

Cooke, H., Lane, A., & Taylor, P. (2018). Open by degrees: A case of flexibility or enhancing education through open degree programs and prior learning assessment. In C. Stevenson (Ed.), *Enhancing education through open degree programs and prior learning assessment* (pp. 128–148). IGI Global. https://doi.org/10.4018/978-1-5225-5255-0.ch008

Davey, T., Meerman, A., Orazbayeva, B., Riedel, M., Galán-Muros, V., Plewa, C., & Eckert, N. (Eds.). (2018). *The future of universities thoughtbook.* University Industry Innovation Network. Retrieved from http://futureuniversities.com/fut_2018-download/

DeYoung, J., & Eberhart, J. C. (Eds.). (2018). *Blended reality: Applied research project—Year 2 report.* Yale. Retrieved from https://blendedreality.yale.edu/news/year-2-report

Ebner, M., & Schön, S. (2018). Open Educational Resources—eine Notwendigkeit für die digital gestützte Hochschullehre. In M. Miglbauer, L. Kieberl, & S. Schmid (Eds.), *Hochschule digital.innovativ* (pp. 183–194). FNMA. Retrieved from https://www.fnma.at/content/download/1529/5759%0AMartin

Eckert, N., Gallenkämper, J., Heiß, H.-U., Kreulich, K., Mooraj, M., Müller, C., ... Spiegelberg, G. (2018). *Smart Germany—Engineering education for the digital transformation* (Discussion Paper for the VDI Quality Dialogue).

European Commission/EACEA/Eurydice. (2018). *The European higher education area in 2018: Bologna process implementation report.* Cham: Education, Audiovisual and Culture Executive Agency. https://doi.org/10.2797/63509

Evans, P., & Wurster, T. S. (1997). Strategy and the new economics of information. *Harvard Business Review.* Retrieved from https://hbr.org/1997/09/strategy-and-the-new-economics-of-information

Facer, K. (2009). *Educational, social and technological futures: A report from the beyond current horizons programme.* Retrieved from https://warwick.ac.uk/fac/soc/ier/publications/2009/beyondcurrenthorizons2009.pdf

Feldstein, M. (2019). *Why Ed Tech will fail to transform education (for now).* Retrieved January 19, 2019, from https://mfeldstein.com/why-ed-tech-will-fail-to-transform-education-for-now/

Georgia Tech. (2018). *Deliberate innovation, lifetime education.* Georgia Tech. Retrieved from http://www.provost.gatech.edu/sites/default/files/documents/deliberate_innovation_lifetime_education.pdf

Gibb, A., Hofer, A.-R., & Klofsten, M. (2018). *The entrepreneurial higher education institution: A review of the concept and its relevance today.* Retrieved from https://heinnovate.eu/sites/default/files/heinnovate_concept_note.pdf

Gilch, H., Beise, A. S., Krempkow, R., Müller, M., Stratmann, F., & Wannemacher, K. (2019). Digitalisierung der Hochschulen. Ergebnisse einer Schwerpunktstudie für die Expertenkommission Forschung und Innovation. EFI. Retrieved from https://www.e-fi.de/fileadmin/Innovationsstudien_2019/StuDIS_14_2019.pdf

Grech, A., & Camilleri, A. F. (2017). *Blockchain in education.* https://doi.org/10.2760/60649

Hall, B. H., & Khan, B. (2003). Adoption of new technology. In *New economy handbook* (pp. 1–19).

Halloran, L., & Friday, C. (2018). *Can the universities of today lead learning for tomorrow?* Retrieved from https://cdn.ey.com/echannel/au/en/industries/government-public-sector/ey-university-of-the-future-2030/EY-university-of-the-future-2030.pdf

Hauschildt, K., Vögtle, E. M., & Gwosć, C. (2018). *Social and economic conditions of student life in Europe.* W. Bertelsmann. https://doi.org/10.3278/6001920cw

Henderikx, P., & Jansen, D. (2018). *The changing pedagogical landscape: In search of patterns in policies and practices of new modes of teaching and learning.* EADTU. Retrieved from eadtu.eu

Hess, N. C. L., Carlson, D. J., Inder, J. D., Jesulola, E., Mcfarlane, J. R., & Smart, N. A. (2016). *World development report 2016: Digital dividends.* The World Bank. https://doi.org/10.1596/978-1-4648-0671-1

Holon IQ. (2018). *Education in 2030—Five scenarios for the future of learning and talent.* Holon IQ. Retrieved from http://www.holoniq.com/wp-content/uploads/2018/06/HolonIQ-Education-in-2030.pdf

Holzer, H. (2015). Job market polarization and US worker skills: A tale of two middles. *Economic Studies.* Retrieved from https://www.brookings.edu/wp-content/uploads/2016/06/polarization_jobs_policy_holzer.pdf

Horn, M. (2018). *WeWork spurs online learning's next step forward.* Retrieved from https://www.forbes.com/sites/michaelhorn/2018/10/04/wework-spurs-online-learnings-next-step-forward/#3127daec2220

Howaldt, J., & Jacobsen, H. (Eds.). (2010). *Soziale Innovation: Auf dem Weg zu einem postindustriellen Innovationsparadigma.* VS Verlag für Sozialwissenschaften.

HRK. (2018). *Die Hochschulen als zentrale Akteure in Wissenschaft und Gesellschaft—Eckpunkte zur Rolle und zu den Herausforderungen des Hochschulsystems.* Retrieved from https://www.hrk.de/fileadmin/redaktion/hrk/02-Dokumente/02-01-Beschluesse/HRK_-_Eckpunkte_HS-System_2018.pdf

Jansen, D., & Konings, L. (2017). *MOOC strategies of European institutions.* EADTU. Retrieved from https://oerknowledgecloud.org/sites/oerknowledgecloud.org/files/MOOC_Strategies_of_European_Institutions.pdf

Jongbloed, B. (2015). Universities as hybrid organizations: Trends, drivers, and challenges for the European university. *International Review of Public Administration, 45*(3), 207–225. https://doi.org/10.1080/00208825.2015.1006027

Kaufmann, D. (Ed.). (2019). *Digitalisierung—Chancen und Herausforderungen für die Universitäten Deutschlands.* DUZ Verlags- und Medienhaus. Retrieved from https://www.duz-special.de/media/baf43cd48414beeb49d9c0f10c201bffdc160028/b2038899609a089f5f5816656316d5b6f52e73e5.pdf

Kelly, A. P., & Hess, F. M. (2013). *Beyond retrofitting—Innovation in higher education.* Hudson Institution Initiative on Future Innovation. Retrieved from http://www.hudson.org/content/researchattachments/attachment/1121/beyond_retrofitting-innovation_in_higher_ed_(kelly-hess,_june_2013).pdf

Kuhn, S., Jungmann, F., Deutsch, K., Drees, P., & Rommens, P. M. (2018). Digitale Transformation der Medizin—Brauchen wir ein Curriculum 4.0 für die Aus-, Fort- und Weiterbildung? *OUP, 7,* 453–458. https://doi.org/10.3238/oup.2018.0453

Livanos, I., & Nunez, I. (2015). Rethinking under-skilling: Evidence from the first Cedefop European skills and jobs survey. In *CEDEFOP/IZA workshop on skills and skill mismatch.* Retrieved from http://conference.iza.org/conference_files/2015_Skill_Mismatch/livanos_i5629.pdf

Manyika, J., Lund, S., Michael, C., Bughin, J., Woetzel, J., Batra, P., … Sanghvi, S. (2017). *Jobs lost, jobs gained: Workforce transitions in a time of automation.* McKinsey Global Institute. Retrieved from https://www.mckinsey.com/~/media/McKinsey/Global_Themes/Future_of_Organizations/What_the_future_of_work_will_mean_for_jobs_skills_and_wages/MGI-Jobs-Lost-Jobs-Gained-Report-December-6-2017.ashx

Masevičiūtė, K., Šaukeckienė, V., & Ozolinčiūtė, E. (2018). *Combining studies and paid jobs—Thematic review.* UAB Araneum. Retrieved from http://www.eurostudent.eu/download_files/documents/TR_paid_jobs.pdf

Michel, A., Baumgartner, P., Brei, C., Hesse, F. W., Kuhn, S., Pohlenz, P., … Spinath, B. (2018). *Framework zur Entwicklung von Curricula im Zeitalter der Digitalen Transformation [Framework for the development of curricula in the age of digital transformation]* (Diskussionspapier No. 1).

Miyazoe, T., & Anderson, T. (2013). Interaction equivalency in an OER, MOOCS and informal learning era. *Journal of Interactive Media in Education,* 1–15. https://doi.org/10.5334/2013-09

Moore, M. G. (1993). Theory of transactional distance. In D. Keegan (Ed.), *Theoretical principles of distance education* (pp. 22–39). Routledge.

Nedelkoska, L., & Quintini, G. (2018). *Automation, skills use and training* (OECD Social, Employment and Migration Working Papers). https://doi.org/10.1787/2e2f4eea-en

OECD. (2008). Four future scenarios for higher education. In *OECD/France international conference higher education to 2030: What futures for quality access in the era of globalisation?* OECD Centre for Educational Research and Innovation. Retrieved from https://www.oecd.org/education/skills-beyond-school/42241931.pdf

OECD. (2016). *Automation and independent work in a digital economy* (Policy brief on the future of work). Retrieved from http://www.oecd.org/employment/emp/Automation-and-independent-work-in-a-digital-economy-2016.pdf

OECD. (2017a). *Key issues for digital transformation in the G20.* OECD Publishing. Retrieved from https://www.de.digital/DIGITAL/Redaktion/EN/Publikation/key-issues-for-digital-transformation-g20.pdf?__blob=publicationFile&v=4

OECD. (2017b). *OECD employment outlook 2017.* OECD Publishing. https://doi.org/10.1787/empl_outlook-2017-en

OECD. (2018). *Education at a glance 2018.* OECD Publishing. https://doi.org/10.1787/eag-2018-en

Orr, D., & Buchem, I. (2019). Digitale Kompetenznachweise für lebenslanges Lernen. Retrieved from https://hochschulforumdigitalisierung.de/de/blog/digitale-kompetenznachweise-fuer-lebenslanges-lernen

Orr, D., & Mishra, S. (2015). A comprehensive approach to investigating the social dimension in European higher education systems—EUROSTUDENT and the PL4SD country reviews. In A. Curaj, L. Matei, R. Pricopie, J. Salmi, & P. Scott (Eds.), *The European higher education area: Between critical reflections and future policies.* Springer.

Orr, D., & Usher, A. (2018). Revisiting student performance as a cornerstone of higher education—How is student performance reflected in performance-based funding? In E. Hazelkorn, H. Coates, & A. C. McCormick (Eds.), *Research handbook on quality, performance and accountability in higher education.* Springer.

Orr, D., van der Hijden, P., Rampelt, F., Röwert, R., & Suter, R. (2018a). *Digitalisation as powerful means for the Bologna Process in European higher education to meet its goals.* Retrieved from https://www.iau-tech.net/single-post/2018/04/09/Digitalisation-as-powerful-means-for-the-Bologna-Process-in-European-higher-education-to-meet-its-goals

Orr, D., van der Hijden, P., Rampelt, F., Röwert, R., & Suter, R. (2018b). *Position paper "Bologna digital".* Retrieved from https://bolognadigital.blog/paper/

Orr, D., Weller, M., & Farrow, R. (2018). *Models for online, open, flexible and technology enhanced higher education across the globe—A comparative analysis.* International Council for Open and Distance Education. Retrieved from https://oofat.oerhub.net/OOFAT/wp-content/uploads/2018/04/Models-report-April-2018_final.pdf

Reich, J., & Ruipérez-Valiente, J. A. (2019). The MOOC pivot. *Science, 363*(6423), 130–131. https://doi.org/10.1126/science.aav7958

Reinmann, G. (2015). *Studientext Didaktisches Design.* Universität Hamburg. Retrieved from https://gabi-reinmann.de/wp-content/uploads/2013/05/Studientext_DD_Sept2015.pdf

Rüede, D., & Lurtz, K. (2012). Mapping the various meanings of social innovation: Towards a differentiated understanding of an emerging concept. *EBS Business School Research Paper Series, 12,* 1–51. https://doi.org/10.2139/ssrn.2091039

Schön, S., Ebner, M., & Schön, M. (2016). *Verschmelzung von digitalen und analogen Lehr- und Lernformaten.* Retrieved from https://hochschulforumdigitalisierung.de/sites/default/files/dateien/HFD_AP_Nr25_Verschmelzung_Digitale_Analoge_Lernformate.pdf

Sharples, M., De Roock, R., Ferguson, R., Gaved, M., Herodotou, C., Koh, E., … Wong, L. H. (2016). *Innovating pedagogy 2016 exploring new forms of teaching, learning and assessment, to guide educators and policy makers.* https://doi.org/10.13140/RG.2.2.20677.04325

Sollosy, M., Guidice, R. M., & Parboteeah, K. P. (2015). A contemporary examination of the miles and snow strategic typology through the lens of ambidexterity. In *Academy of Management Proceedings* (Vol. 2015). https://doi.org/10.5465/AMBPP.2015.11213abstract

Südekum, J. (2018). *Digitalisierung und die Zukunft der Arbeit* (No. 19). Retrieved from http://www.wpz-fgn.com/wp-content/uploads/PA19DigitalisierungZukunftArbeit20180726.pdf

Taddei, F. (2018). *Un plan pour co-construire une société apprenante.* Centre de recherches interdisciplinaires (CRI). Retrieved from https://cri-paris.org/wp-content/uploads/2018/04/Un-plan-pour-co-contruire-une-societe-apprenante.pdf

Ubachs, G., Konings, L., & Brown, M. (Eds.). (2017). *The envisioning report for empowering universities.* EADTU. Retrieved from http://empower.eadtu.eu/images/report/The_Envisioning_Report_for_Empowering_Universities_1st_edition_2017.pdf

Unger, M., & Zaussinger, S. (2018). *Background paper—The new student: Flexible learning paths and future learning environments.* Institute for Advanced Studies. Retrieved from https://www.eu2018.at/dam/jcr:9998b09f-3e5d-439f-9c1f-e959f3ef649d/Background_paper_(not_available_in_an_accessible_format)_(EN).pdf

United Nations. (2015). *Transforming our world by 2030: A new agenda for global action* (Zero draft of the outcome document for the UN Summit to adopt the post-2015 development agenda). Retrieved from https://sustainabledevelopment.un.org/content/documents/1819BN_2_26_June_final.pdf

Universities UK. (2018). *Solving future skills challenges.* Universities UK. Retrieved from https://www.universitiesuk.ac.uk/policy-and-analysis/reports/Pages/solving-future-skills-challenges.aspx

van der Wende, M. (2017). *Opening up: Higher education systems in global perspective* (No. 22). Retrieved from http://www.researchcghe.org/perch/resources/publications/wp22.pdf

van der Zwaan, B. (2017). *Higher education in 2040. A global approach.* Amsterdam University Press. Retrieved from http://www.oapen.org/search?identifier=625978;keyword=higher education

Wannemacher, K. (2016). *Digitale Lernszenarien im Hochschulbereich* (Geschäftsstelle Hochschulforum Digitalisierung, Ed.) (Arbeitspapier Nr. 15). Edition Stifterverband. Retrieved from https://hochschulforumdigitalisierung.de/sites/default/files/dateien/HFD_AP_Nr15_Digitale_Lernszenarien.pdf

Wissenschaftsrat. (2010). *Empfehlungen zur Differenzierung der Hochschulen.* Wissenschaftsrat. Retrieved from https://www.wissenschaftsrat.de/download/archiv/10387-10.pdf

Zenhäusern, P., & Vaterlaus, S. (2017). *Digitalisierung und Arbeitsmarktfolgen—Metastudie zum Stand der Literatur und zu den Entwicklungen in der Schweiz.* Fondation CH2048. Retrieved from https://www.ch2048.ch/pics/files/Polynomics_Arbeitsmarktfolgen_Bericht_20170621a.pdf

Zick, M., & Heinrich, S. (2018). Learning analytics als Instrument zur qualitativen Weiterentwicklung und Flexibilisierung von Studium und Lehre. *Forum Neue Medien in der Lehre Austria, 1,* 12–14.